Women Entrepreneur

Prayers

Strategic Prayers to Rebrand Your Life and Business

Volume 1

Visionary Author
Darlene Higgs Hollis

McDonough, Georgia, U.S.A.

Woman Entrepreneur Prayers

Dedicated to Pastor Cassandra Elliott, affectionately known as "Pastor C", "Coach C" or "PC" to those she loved and mentored. Thank you for the lessons you taught us while you were here on earth with us.

Acknowledgments

I want to take this time out to thank my children for allowing me the space to complete this assignment. I appreciate your sacrifices and grace you gave me while I worked long hours on this assignment.

To the co-authors, thank you for going on this assignment journey with me. Thank you for trusting me and accepting the charge. Your efforts, pour and sacrifice are greatly appreciated.

To the ten women that prayed during the Prayer Huddle that this book was birthed from, thank you for accepting the assignment and getting on with me those early mornings for five days. Then agreeing when God said, "Now write a book!"

To my team and administrators thank you for your hard work, dedication and diligence. Special thanks to Tenishia, Shaundra, Elisha and Ronisa. Ronisa and Tenishia, thank you for your extra push from the inception of this book to the end as I worked out articulating the vision of this book and events to follow.

To everyone that has kept us all lifted in prayer, your prayers were needed and felt.

To the person that will pick up this book, I pray a fresh wind be blown upon your life and business. May God strengthen, fortify and give you laser focus to carry out the assignment over your life. Though winds blow and distractions come, you will not be moved. I declare you are planted like a tree by water according to Psalms 1:3 (AMP)

Most importantly but certainly not least, I want to thank God for the assignment. Though I may not always understand or grasp the full impact of why God has me embark on a particular journey and assignment, obedience is what He looks for and honors. I will always steward well—the assignments, people and charges of the Lord.

Foreword

by Doretha Rivers-McClinton

Women Entrepreneur Prayers: Strategic Prayers to Rebrand Your Life and Business is an awesome book! Know that in the timing of God concerning business aspects, that God will truly answer and perfect that concerning your life.

I highly recommend this book to women that have a vision of and purpose for their dream. God will bring it into full circle. Never give up on it. Know that it's working for your good.

I'm reminded of my book *Push Until Something Happens: If you work it, it will work for you*. If you ask God for something, never be afraid to ask BIG. That's the treasure to your success.

Use these strategic prayers to help you through those challenging times in your business.

- Doretha Rivers-McClinton
Pastor, Apostle, Prophetess, CEO
Author of: *If You Work it, it Will Work For You: The Treasures to Your Success*; *Entering into the Presence of God: Push Until Something Happens Holding on to the Horns of the Altar*, *I Can't Go Any Further Until I Do It: Activate Your Faith Now and Experience Authentic Living*

Table of Contents

Visionary Author Note

As Christian women business owners, we can't help but find ways to reconcile our faith with our marketplace ministry. Within our own businesses, we no longer feel the need to check our faith at the door and pretend that everything we do is in our own strength and power. For us to be successful, get new ideas, find new strategies, and just find strength to not quit—we rely on our faith.

Prayer has brought me to this point in my business. I prayed many days when I felt like throwing in the towel. I prayed when I needed direction on creating or launching an offer. There were also those days when I needed a new strategy, or even to know where to invest.

However, though we pray, many times, our prayers don't have structure so that we can effectively pray over our businesses. Or sometimes we don't even think that God is concerned with the intricate working of our businesses, so we don't bring these concerns to him.

So, at the beginning of this year, I got some of my intercessor, prayer warrior, entrepreneur friends together to form a Prayer Huddle. For five days, we showed up on Zoom and Clubhouse at six-thirty A.M. and prayed for specific prayer points. We invited other women to come on and pray these prayers for their businesses as well. These five days were so powerful and transformational that we agreed to put those prayers in print.

The prayers within this book give you language to strategically pray for specific areas where your life and business meet. This book is a tool that you can pick up and turn to the prayer that you need at that moment. Each prayer is written so that you can repeat that prayer and pray over yourself.

Each prayer is written by a woman who is an expert or well-versed in the focus of that prayer.

I pray this book changes your life and business; that you become more confident in your marketplace assignment.

Mind

A Step of Faith

Tenishia Lester

JOSHUA 3:1-17 (AMP)

Context: The Levitical Priests were the only ones allowed to carry the Ark of the Covenant. The Ark of the Covenant represented God's presence and power. At the time of crossing the Jordan, it was Spring, a time when the water levels were high and reached flood levels.

When we consider mindsets and business, what comes to mind are the following:

- We undercut our prices
- Undervalue ourselves and our services
- Feel unworthy; lack confidence
- Operate in stagnation and procrastination
- Think no one will purchase what we offer
- Think no one will support us

These are a few hallmarks of negative mindsets. As Christian business owners, often business is viewed as a ministry only. The biggest misconception is that as a Christian (and a Christian woman at that) you cannot operate in the marketplace and ministry. NOT SO! You can seamlessly mesh the two, leaving no parts of you to the side—showing up as completely YOU!

In the scripture above, Joshua 3, (AMP), during my study time, God spoke to me concerning mindsets and acting in faith. Here is what I gleaned: We allow our negative mindsets to hinder us. How many times have you prayed for an answer or instructions from God concerning next steps to cross over into your "Business Promised Land?" I know I have prayed many times! Many times, He has given me the next step or instruction, but when I cannot see how it will play out or I lack faith in what I am about to embark upon, my faith wanes. And what do we do when there is a lack of confidence in our skills or services? We stand still and do not move?

I am guilty of such! If I cannot fathom how it will play out, or if I do not have all I deem to be necessary action steps, I fail to move. My lack of action has caused me to lose money, feel frustrated, angry, and even stagnant. I have gotten better, but honestly, there are still some occasions when I do not move in a timely fashion.

Now whether fear or procrastination is the cause for the lack of movement, (it's the fear and lack of control for me) you must evaluate. However, that does not mean instructions were not given and prayers were not answered. The parting of the sea occurs when we obediently act on the instructions that God has given us. It's the stepping out on faith and into the waters of drowning proportions that God has you. It is taking the first step and allowing God to "part the river" i.e., open doors and make ways. Then the blessings are opened for us to cross over into the Promised Land.

If you look back, what you will find is that God gave you a set of instructions to follow. Just as Joshua instructed the Levites who were carrying the Ark of the Covenant and the Israelites. The Jordan appeared to be impassable—the threat of drowning was real, their faith may have been shaky, and their confidence may have been lacking. But when they followed the instructions given and stepped in faith, the Jordan parted, and dry land appeared which allowed them to cross over safely to the Promised Land.

So, what blessings have you not been able to walk into because of your mindset and not following the path that God has laid out for you? What instructions have you ignored? What first step into the water have you not taken? What prophetic words are looming over your head that you are questioning God about and wondering will they ever manifest?

Here are some practical steps to consider after you have answered the questions above:

1. Pray and ask God to reveal what instructions you missed.
2. Examine your negative mindsets and the possible root causes.
3. Revisit your instruction.
4. Write an action plan.
5. What is one action that you can take immediately?

Prayer

Father, in the name of Jesus, I come to you now as your daughter, bowing down and humble before you. I thank you for who you are and repent for being disobedient and not following your instructions. I repent for not having enough faith in you to act on the instructions you have given me. Thank you for the instructions, that I can follow them and use them to move forward into who I am and who you've called me to be. Father, I repent oh God for a mindset that is not like you. May the refiners fire purify our hearts and purify our minds so that I can walk circumspectly, boldly and powerfully into who you have called me to be. I declare that I AM a Kingdom business owner. I declare that I will lean not on my own understanding of the things that I don't see God, but the things that you already ordained and called me to be. According to Psalms 139, when you knew me, formed me and knitted me in my mother's womb. God, you know the end from the beginning. Father, while I may not be able to see beyond my mindset of comparison and my mindset of being unworthy and my mindset stagnation, I will follow you and step out in discomfort as an act of faith. Father, I symbolically hand you my articles of registration for my business(es) I turn them over to you right now in the name of Jesus Father, declaring and decreeing that my business(es) is/are yours God.

I declare and decree you are the CEO of my business(es). God allow me to be a good steward of your business. I thank you Father for creativity, for divine downloads, witty inventions, proper staffing of my life and business and wisdom as you crowned Solomon with wisdom in the name of Jesus. I thank you for each person that has been called to my voice and for tuning my ears to your voice because your word says that your sheep know your voice and no other will they follow. In the name of Jesus, I declare that I hear you and I hear you clearly, renew my mind, open my ears and my heart. I pray that you get the glory from my life and businesses. I thank you, Father God and seal this prayer with your precious blood. In Jesus name, Amen.

I Changed My Mind

TuRhonda Freeman

Then the LORD replied: "Write down the revelation and make it plain on tablets so that a herald may run with it.
-Habakkuk 2:2 (NIV)

D
o you believe in the transformational power of vision? Do you believe that there is a God-vision made specifically for you?

Do you believe that there is a vision that can shift the very trajectory of your business in a real and personal way?

The one thing the Bible tells us about vision comes from Habakkuk 2:2 (NKJV)

Then the Lord answered me and said:

"Write the vision and make it plain on tablets, that he may run who reads it.

In the first chapter of Habakkuk, the prophet went to God about the increasing injustices in the society. He was concerned that God had turned a blind eye to what was happening all around him. Habakkuk presented two complaints to the LORD: How long shall I cry, and You will not hear? (Habakkuk 1:2 NKJV) and Why do You show me iniquity and cause me to see trouble? (Habakkuk 1:3 NKJV)

These two questions plagued Habakkuk's heart: How long? Why?

Aren't these the same two questions that haunt us when the circumstances of life seem to close in on us, with no detectable end in sight? Aren't these the same two questions we ask when we've been praying for the same thing for a seemingly long time? Aren't these the same two questions we ask when God has put us in the waiting room—and we see everyone else being called up for their blessing, yet He keeps us waiting?

When God responded to Habakkuk (because God always responds, whether we see it or not), He told him to "Look among the nations and watch! Be utterly astounded! For I will work a work in your days which you would not believe, though it were told you." (Habakkuk 1:5 NKJV)

What is God doing in your midst that you may have failed to see?

Allow me to encourage you with the same words that God spoke to Habakkuk.

- Look! Open up your spiritual eyes to see that God has not forgotten about you.
- Watch! Pay close attention to what He is doing in and through you.
- Be astonished! Be literally dumbfounded and filled with amazement for the vision that He is giving you.

The right vision has a way of changing your mind. The second time Habakkuk prayed; his tone was completely different. "I will stand my watch and set myself on the rampart and watch to see what He will say to me, and what I will answer when I am corrected. (Habakkuk 2:1 NKJV)

His changed mind resulted from a new vantage point. He climbed up on a rampart, which was similar to a tower set high above the city. He positioned himself high enough to have a strategic view of all the movements on the ground.

What would you be able to see if your vantage point was different?

What could you manifest in your business if you went higher in your thinking, believing, praying and confessing?

When Habakkuk went up higher, God responded in a way that changed the trajectory of his life.

Then the LORD answered me and said: Write the vision, and make it plain on tablets, that he may run who reads it.

For the vision is yet for an appointed time; but at the end it will speak, and it will not lie. Though it tarries, wait for it; because it will surely come, it will not tarry. Habbakuk 2:2 (NKJV)

My granny used to say, "Nothing can stop a woman with a made-up mind." Today, let's change our minds and climb up higher, so we can see the God-vision tailor made for us.

REPEAT AFTER ME:

- *Today, I changed my mind.*

- *I'm not satisfied with being behind, beneath, or below. I was created for the top.*

- *I'm not satisfied with having barely enough. I will live and work in abundance.*

- *I'm not satisfied with being average. I am surrounded by extraordinary favor.*

- *I'm not satisfied with mediocrity in my business. I work with a spirit of excellence.*

- *I'm not satisfied with being put in a box. I will break every mold and defy every odd.*

- *I declare that I will overcome every obstacle, boundary, limitation, hindrance, and challenge.*

- *Nothing can stop me because I changed my mind.*

  And it is so. Amen!

Diligence

Shaundra Straughter

Do you see someone skilled in their work? They will serve before kings; they will not serve before officials of low rank.
Proverbs 22:29 (NIV)

The rituals and routines of everyday living can influence the amount of effort we put into our businesses. It is important that we do not become weary in the ebb and flow of providing and sustaining until we allow outside elements to control our input and output. I know, it is easier said than done. How many times have you found yourself on the struggle bus to get moving towards your goals and plans because of the fatigue decision-making brings? Maybe your nine-to-five drains you until there is nothing to give towards your endeavors for entrepreneurship. The complexity of finding balance in prioritizing life's many distractions and obligations will cause us to become delusional in our focus and faithfulness to our assignments. Regardless, we have been called to be diligent in all things.

Proverbs 12:24 (NIV) encourages us to remain diligent in our work. When we become committed to diligence, we are guaranteed to become sharp in our skills and increase our influence in the marketplace and on those connected to us. Being diligent allows us to build, lead, and impact at a greater level of consistency and sustainability. It is easy to remain diligent in our work when we naturally love what we have been called to. If we are struggling in our businesses, we must reflect on our call. We must consider our "why." Become intimate with our pillars for establishing our business and recommit to the work that is at hand. We must not become "weary in our well-doing because we shall reap in due season if we faint not" (Galatians 6:9 KJV).

When we remain diligent in our work, we will truly exemplify Proverbs 22:29 (NIV), "Do you see someone skilled in their work? They will serve before kings; they will not serve before officials of low rank." Our commitment to our work, our dedication to strengthening the craft of our hands, and willingness to share the creativities of our heart will lead us to places beyond our current level of thinking. We will surpass any limitation that previously held us bound. Where you are today is not where you will be tomorrow. No one and nothing can stop the elevation that will come because of your hard work and sacrifice. The only catalyst that can prohibit or delay us from getting to where we have been called is slothfulness—pure laziness. I encourage you to continue to rise and shine on this journey. Be diligent even when it feels as though the prize is nowhere in sight. You shall be triumphant because you will choose diligence in all things!

Prayer

Dear Heavenly Father,

I am coming before you today to tell you thank you for choosing me for this assignment. Thank you for considering me worthy to complete the work that you have placed in my hands. God, I ask you to forgive me if I have shown complacency in any area of my life and business. Give me strength to continue to seek your face and your wisdom in all things. Help me to be a good steward over my gifts, my finances, and my connections. Help me to accept and cultivate the ideas you download within me. Let my hands not be found idle, entertaining laziness. Continue to prepare me for all aspects of this journey God. I believe that you will finish the work that you have begun in me. I am destined to stand before queens and kings. My diligence shall speak on my behalf. You are preparing national and international rooms for me because you can trust me. Thank you now for allowing my gift to make room for me. I will remain dedicated to the work and steadfast in You, in Jesus' name. Amen.

Run Your Race: Be Your Own Competition

Darlene Higgs Hollis

Since we have such a huge crowd of men of faith watching us from the grandstands, let us strip off anything that slows us down or holds us back, and especially those sins that wrap themselves so tightly around our feet and trip us up; and let us run with patience the particular race that God has set before us.

Hebrews 12:1 (TLB)

As we are out here in these entrepreneurial streets, we experience so much pressure to follow along with the current trends; especially as it pertains to social media. We feel the need to do what everybody seems to be doing successfully. We worry we will lose our audience or there will be no growth if we don't follow these trends. But for most of us, we get fatigued and overwhelmed, trying to do whatever everyone seems to be doing.

I've felt this pressure many times, even though I am one who prefers to blaze my own trail versus going with the status quo. One day, in my quiet time, I heard the voice of the Lord say to me, "Run your own race! Be your own competition!" I felt such peace. I felt centered and ready to continue doing business the way God instructed me.

My sister, today I tell you, run your race! Don't look at what others are doing. Don't worry about people not wanting to use your services or buy your products anymore because you are not doing what everyone else is. Keep looking steadily ahead. Like Hebrews 12:1 says, run your race with patience; the race that God gave to you and assigned you to. There are still clients out there who need you. Many more. Your assignment is to them, and only them. Don't let what you see discourage you.

The success that you think you see others experiencing is sometimes just an illusion; you are not privy to the behind-the-scenes and the real story. So, stay focused on your race. Many times, who you think is the competition is not really a competition.

Run your race at the pace that is set for you. Ecclesiastes 9:11 reminds us that the race is not won by the swiftest. Be comfortable with your assignment and how you are to create and work it. Be your own competition. Compare your accomplishments with your goals. The persons assigned to you will support and glean from the authentic you.

Prayer

Lord, I come to you today, thanking you for trusting me with this assignment to make a difference in the lives of others. As I am working on this assignment, I ask you to help me shut out the noise of performing what does not feel authentically me. Please help me to not lose myself and become overwhelmed. I want to grow, be more visible so that others can find me, and I serve them, but I also don't want to feel as if I am doing things only to keep up with the trend. Help me to focus only on what you tell me to do, and how you tell me to do it. Help me hear your voice even as others I trust guide me. I need your help to discern what is coming from you so that I can take action. As I walk out this assignment, help me to be at peace when I don't follow trends, or do what my peers are doing. Help me to be laser-focused on the path that you are having me to create. Lord, whenever I veer from running my race, please send me a reminder to get back on my path. I thank you in advance for helping me to run my race with confidence knowing that you are with me. In your name Jesus I pray. Amen.

A Mindset
of Fear

Tenishia Lester

Casting all your cares [all your anxieties, all your worries, and all your concerns, once and for all] on Him, for He cares about you [with deepest affection, and watches over you very carefully].
1 Peter 5:7 (AMP)

Fear is probably the most common emotion and hinderance for business owners that can be spread across many facets of life that have implications in business. The first aspect that we all most commonly encounter is the fear of your ability to be a businesswoman. I know that was my initial response. I had no clue what it would take to run and maintain a business. If that is you, you are in good company. There are others, conversely, that starting a business may have been an easy decision, and I applaud you. There are a varied number of scenarios that we can play out in our minds that give credence to our fears.

Fear of:

- Success/Failure
- Lack of knowledge
- Lack of support/connections
- Insufficient financing

- Lack of equipment

The list can go on— in fact jot down any fears now that arise for you, that I may not have listed.

We tend to discount the fears that we deal with in life and the implications that they have in business. You will most likely act and react from that place. The effects will be visible even though it may not be a conscious act. This is where being aware of your fears and the root causes is important. You will want to mitigate triggers where you can.

The key question that needs to be asked, that I often ask myself, is "Are you going to allow your fears to stop you?" If your answer is 'no', then ask yourself, "What do I need to do to overcome or minimize my fear in this area?"

How can you face your fear and use it as fuel? You may just find that the solution to the problem was within your reach all along. Or there may be a trusted individual that you can have a conversation with, who may have the answer for you or can point you in the right direction.

It is often easy to get caught up as businesswomen in comparing our journeys to that of others. Not everyone will be honest to state this, but it happens. We compare our current or beginning chapters to that which may be the second edition of another businesswoman. That is a situation that will never bode well. Truth of the matter is, you do not know what it took for her to reach that level of success. How many times did she fail? What did she have to sacrifice? What did she have to endure? What did she know or not know?

Identifying the correct audience is another fear that may impact your business. You must do your due diligence to ensure that you are serving or reaching the proper people. Otherwise, you can face many days of trial and error. Not that finding your audience immediately you will not have to try various strategies or tools and adjust where necessary. But you cannot be afraid to try and fail. It is in those "failing" moments that we learn how to hone our products and services to be the most efficient they can be.

In 1 Peter 5:7, it says to cast your cares on God. This means we are to take everything—no matter how minute you may feel it is—to God. There is nothing that He is not concerned about, especially if it is a concern to you. I think this is where we get off track and allow those fears to take control; because we think that we can achieve success in our own strength and ability.

Don't get me wrong your talents and gifts will take you places, but we all need the strength, power, favor, instruction, wisdom and grace of God to assist us along the way as well. Many only look to God when there is trouble on the horizon. How much faith do we have daily while operating a business? So, I want to ask you, do you really include God in your processes by taking the time out to pray as a business owner?

It is easy to slip into a routine and begin trying to make things happen on our own accord as business owners. Especially, when circumstances appear to be going well. Other tasks begin to take precedence over having a conversation with God about our businesses.

We should be including God in our processes and giving God our businesses wholeheartedly daily so that we can not only operate, not only in ministry but also in the marketplace for His glory.

Each day has enough trouble unto itself according to Matt. 6:34 which is the most perfect reason to cast cares daily. Are you taking the time out to have a conversation with God about your business for the day? Are you being anxious for nothing but with prayer and supplication making your request known? And when I say conversation, I mean not just you are talking. Are you listening for a response to gain the knowledge and wisdom to proceed?

You should know that you have the power to do and execute anything that God places in your hands. Everything may not always go as you plan or hope, but you can do it because He has bestowed upon you the power and a sound mind to execute.

Scripture References: Matthew 6:34 (AMP); Philippians 4:6 (AMP); 2 Timothy 1:7 (AMP)

Prayer

Father, I repent for being fearful and not leaning on you for the power you so freely give, to execute that which you have given unto me. I believe that you can do all things and I can do all things with you. Help me to turn my fears into fuel. Help me to identify the roots of my fears so that I may be able to heal in those areas. Allow my focus to be centered on my race and not those around me. I declare that what I have to offer the world is uniquely mine. My perspective is relevant, necessary and sought after. Thank you for the creativity to operate well. Allow the ears of those tuned to my voice to find me. Allow those that have words specific to my journey and ear to be found by me. Staff my life and business appropriately so that you receive all of the glory from (insert your name and business name here.) _____. I come out of agreement with every negative word/thought that I have spoken about (my business name) _____ and myself as the business owner, in Jesus' name. I renounce my fears of (speak every fear and negative word you have spoken) _____, in Jesus' name. I declare and decree life, prosperity, longevity, success, and wealth over (business name) _____, myself, my staff and my customers/clientele, in Jesus' name. Cover my business(es) with your blood and lead me daily, it is in your name I pray Amen.

Vision

Elisha Lison

*Where there is no vision, the people perish: but he that keepeth the law,
happy is he.*
Proverbs 29:18 (KJV)

According to Oxford Dictionary, vision means "to have the ability to think about or plan the future with imagination or wisdom". Everything that you see around you first started with a vision. Everything that has been materialized started in someone's mind before they could manifest it into reality. This works the same way in our lives and in business. If you want something to happen in your life, you must be able to imagine it first. When we walk through life without a vision, then we are just wandering, and it is hard, or even impossible, to intentionally manifest what we want to see happen.

When I first started my journey in entrepreneurship, I struggled with envisioning exactly how I saw things manifesting, who I wanted to reach, and what I wanted my business to evolve into. This was a huge problem because it stopped me from moving forward whenever it was time to decide. This was one of the biggest reasons I thought my business would eventually fail because of my inability to literally see things through. I realized I had a struggling belief system; a part of me believed I was made to be an entrepreneur, while a part of me also believed that I didn't have the vision to even imagine something that I could manifest into this world.

After I became serious about my journey to know God, I realized He created us in His image, and He is the ultimate creator, so there was no way possible that He left me with no ability to envision. It just made little sense once I knew the truth about my Creator and learned the truth about who He created me to be. I tore down the limiting belief system that had taken root inside of me and was hindering me from moving forward. Proverbs 29:18 tells us, "Where there is no vision, the people perish." This set me free from the lie that I had no vision and shined a light on the truth that God has given us vision and imagination to manifest. God did not put us on earth to see us perish, but to have everlasting life. His Word also tells us He has plans for us to give us a future and a hope.

After learning this truth, I stood up against the blockage that came up every time I attempted to envision my future or my business. Vision empowers you with the ability to be intentional and clearly sees the goals that you need to accomplish to get to where you want to go. I challenge you to sit down and visualize the direction that you want your life and your business to go and then create goals that align with that vision. Set splinter goals, which are smaller goals, to get to the big goals and set a timeframe in which you would like to accomplish it. Fear may try to come up and stop you in your tracks but do not give in and do not let up! You were not given the spirit of fear but the spirit of love, power, and a sound mind. You were created to do the things that God has placed in your mind and heart to accomplish. Go get it!

Prayer

Father,

I ask you to break every limiting belief system and struggling belief system that does not reflect who you have made me to be. I ask that you set my imagination free and give me the vision to see through your eyes and not just mine. I ask that you bless my mind to be strategic and my hands to be fruitful to bring forth every vision that you have given me for my life and business. I rebuke anything that is trying to step in the way of the things that you have given me to accomplish. Everything that is trying to hinder my business from being successful I step over it right now. In Jesus' name I pray. Amen.

Pushing Past the Stress!

Ronisa Glass

Be careful for nothing; but in everything by prayer and supplication with thanksgiving let your requests be made known unto God. And the peace of God, which passeth all understanding, shall keep your hearts and minds through Christ Jesus.
Philippians 4: 6-7 (KJV)

It can be hard to push, pause, and then pursue the very thing you know you were destined to do. Anything that God gives you is worth fighting for! That is the thrust behind purpose. Once you catch the vison, and write it down, you work to execute the plan. What you don't understand, you pray for revelation of it and for wisdom to come. God has predestined you to stand in a place of victory, so get up and get back to work.

Prayer

Lord, I'm tired. I've been under so much stress. I feel like this load gets too heavy for me to carry at times. Right now, it's a little hard. I know I've been worrying, and that's not what you will have me to do. I'm supposed to put it all in your hands. To trust you. Lord, I've tried not to complain, and I've tried not to murmur about my circumstances, nor how things are going. I need your help. Today, I don't feel like I can do it. So, I'm asking for you to help push me a little bit further and then, to pull me through. Lord, I want to lean on you. I know what you called me to do but God, I just need your guidance right now. I don't want to mess things up by trying to do it in my own way or my own strength. Father, show me how to pull back when I need to. Show me how to take refuge in your peace. I do know I can always lean on you. I can trust in you. Lord, I know that I can depend on you. Will you help me see this thing through? Lord, I know that self-care is what I need, for me to be the most productive businesswoman and entrepreneur that I can be. Oh God, help me not to do things in my own way, but to follow your plan and your command concerning my business, my ministry, and my life. I want to be healthy, happy, and whole. Not only in my physical health, but in my mental, emotional, spiritual, financial, and relational health as well. Father, I pray for your hand that covers, leads, and guides me. As tough as it can be sometimes, I am learning how to do self-reflections. I want to be a mirror of your image. I want to be the best that I can be, and I know that I can achieve it by following your plan.

Help me not to be so in control that I lose control. Lord, on this day, I'm going to take a step back so you can step in. I am relinquishing all control so that you can flow. I pray in Jesus' name, for fresh revelation as an entrepreneur and businesswoman, that you have called me to be. Help me to maintain times of self-reflection, so that I can always project the right attitude and focus. Father, I want to be responsible with what you have given me. I want to plan breaks accordingly, so that I can always maintain the appropriate visibility and the right spirit. Thank you, Lord, for giving me this business and for making me the kingdom entrepreneur that you have called me to be. Today oh

God, I take back my strength and power. I take back my peace and my joy. I stand fully on your word and your promises concerning me, my business and all that I hold dear. I will let go of everything that tries to bring on frustrations or to cause me to worry or stress. Today, I take my hands off, and I put it all in your hands. I know with you at the forefront, the spirit of wholeness will come and be my portion. Being whole in you means everything will come together for the good. I am your vessel, Lord. Fill me, replenish me and revive me again.

In Jesus' Name. Amen!

Healing

Elisha Lison

And be not conformed to this world: but be ye transformed by the renewing of your mind, that ye may prove what is that good, and acceptable, and perfect, will of God.
Romans 12:2 (KJV)

Healing has been such an important part of my journey because I realized that when you have not healed from the past, it will taint everything you attempt to do. Out of your heart pours your creativity, so if your heart is tainted with hurt, pain, bitterness and unforgiveness, you are blocking your creativity from running free. Have you ever noticed that when you are your happiest, your creativity runs wild? The same goes for your mind. When your mind is a mess, after a while everything else will follow. When your mind is clear, you can think clearly and having a clean heart gives your creativity the ability to run free. With both a clean heart and mind, you can pour from a clear and healthy space.

Previously, as I attempted to start my first business, I was doing it with a tainted heart and a mess for a mind. Naturally, my business reflected my heart posture and state of mind, so my business was short-lived.

After journeying with God, I realized that my mind was bogged down with a hindering belief system from experiences and outcomes. I never even truly believed that my business could be successful, even though I poured resources and endless time into making it appear to be. I had conformed to the world and our generation of instant success and pictures worthy of no meaningful substance. After realizing that it wasn't my business idea or strategy that was the problem, but it was my mind that needed correcting, this scripture gave me so much revelation. This scripture is significant to healing because once you have been renewed in your mind (healed from past belief systems that has infected your heart and your faith, you can move forward with the plans for your business and life healthily), when you have transformed your mind from what the world has taught you and what the enemy has told you, you can finally think from a clear space which will give you creativity unmatched. This will also give you the ability to see the areas where your heart is out of alignment with God. You will be more cognizant of when you are pouring from hurt or bitterness instead of love and wholeness. You'll be able to show up as the person God has created you to be and with the mind of Christ and not be double minded. Transforming your mind will give you the ability to stand on God's words and believe the truth that He has given you all you need for what He has called you to do.

Prayer

Father God,

In the name of Jesus, I pray you allow your words to transform my mind and break down every belief system that is hindering me from being who you have called me to be and from doing all that you have called me to do. I ask that you empower me with the Holy Spirit to move at the capacity and momentum I need to be successful and to be excellent in all you have called me to accomplish. I ask that you search my heart and remove anything that does not reflect you and give me a clean heart and clear mind. In Jesus' mighty name I pray. Amen.

Fear of Rejection

Tenishia Lester

He came unto his own, and they that were his own received him not.
John 1:11 (ASV)

I have experienced being rejected many times throughout my life; rejected by family, friends, career, men and in business. It is a position that causes much discomfort, hurt, and pain. It leads to mistrust and fear. Can you imagine walking through life just waiting for someone to reject you? Not that everyone rejected me, but it only took a few instances for it to feel like the norm for me and caused me to close off my heart.

Consequently, I developed a victim mentality; always waiting for the other shoe to drop. Always blaming others for my situations and circumstances. Others were to blame for why I did not accomplish things I set out to do. Have you ever made the statement "If only others would/could...?" That is a dangerous statement. Why? Because you place your power in the hands of others. Why relinquish your power when you can harness it for good?

My rejection looked like: not applying again for jobs I qualified for and feeling trapped, not pursuing education, seeking the wrong relationships, cutting off family members, and feeling like I couldn't be a successful entrepreneur. It was easier for me to be a good steward of the vision for others than to use those same ideas for myself. It looked like I was remaining in the background because I didn't want to be seen or heard.

What does rejection look like for you?

Here is the hard truth: not everyone will love you, love your ideas, see you, value you, understand you, want to be around you, buy from you, celebrate you, listen to you, or support you; the list can go on. The point is because I anticipated what rejection would look like, it became a hinderance.

Though I worked on healing my heart from rejection, now and then it resurfaces. Two of the areas it shows most are relationships and business. I easily overthink and get into my head, therefore manufacturing a million reasons someone will not buy or want what I offer. Fear of rejection is why I feel that I will not find someone to love me for who I am and be my complement. Added to this, yes, I feel there are those that will not purchase my coaching services, books, or offerings and those that I should not be in relation with. Yet, there are people that will want my services. And there is someone that God has made just for me.

In times where rejection begins to surface for me/you here are a few things to remember:

1. As scripture says they rejected Jesus. His own people no less.
2. Ask yourself is there any truth to your thought pattern?
3. Though you may not be for everyone, you are for someone.
4. What you have to offer the world is valuable.

5. You matter!

6. Start the business. Write the book.

7. Though the idea may not be successful the first time reevaluate and try again.

And most important of all, YOU WERE CREATED ON PURPOSE WITH A PURPOSE! PRECIOUS AND CHOSEN!

Scripture references: Isaiah 53:3 (NLT); 1Peter 2:4 (ESV)

Prayer

Father in the name of Jesus, help me when rejection rears its ugly head. Allow me to not wallow in the past and erect a barrier around my heart that keeps anyone from climbing over or around. Allow me to see the truth of a situation. Teach me how to trust again, teach me how to love again, teach me how to see the good in others and myself. Show me who you created me to be and allow me to walk in that comfortably. Reaffirm that I am valuable and that what I have to say, and offer are valuable and needed. Allow my heart to be open to love. Teach me to include you in my business and to see you as the CEO. Teach me to take risks and be okay with things not working the first time. Allow me to learn from my failures and try again. I thank you that my voice is attuned to a people that you have set aside just for me. Allow me to not be afraid to be seen so that my voice amplifies in the earth as you intended it to be. Teach me not to shrink back when I feel uncomfortable. I thank you that I can lean on you when I feel weak and unsure. I thank you for ordering my steps and giving me grace when I falter. Father, I know that you are sufficient in my insufficiency. You are strong when I am weak.

Though others may reject me I know that you will always welcome me with open arms. And for that I bless, honor and give you praise. Amen.

SPIRIT

Doing Business God's Way

Dr. Janine Graham-Howard

But thou shalt remember the Lord thy God for it is he that giveth thee power to get wealth, that he may establish his covenant which he swore unto thy fathers, as it is this day.
Deuteronomy 8:18 (KJV)

All our skills and talents that we use in our businesses/ministries are all given to us by God. God gives us the ability to make money, to make deals, and to obtain wealth. The one thing we must realize is we have to use the Bible as a learning tool for God's principles to create, expand, and maintain our businesses. So, when we look and read the Word of God, we can get the natural power that lies within us to develop for our successes.

The Bible tells us in Mark 12:17 (NLT), give to Caesar what belongs to Caesar and give to God what belongs to God. Then Psalms 24:1 (NIV) says, "The earth is the Lord's and the fullness thereof and they that dwell therein." Since your business is in the earth, your business belongs to God. So why not take all the directions from God since your business belongs to God?

It's all about God. All our destinies, goals, and desires should be about God. We should always live for His purpose, not our own but His purpose for our life and business endeavors. Our businesses should glorify the Father. God never intended for us to handle life on our own, nor did He ever intend for us to handle our businesses and ministries on our own. He's designed us in such a way that we must depend on Him. The Bible tells clearly, to commit thy works unto the Lord and your plans shall be established. (Prov. 16:3 KJV)

If you hear nothing else, I've said, COMMITT it, (your businesses and ministries) unto the Lord so that He can establish them. God wants to take all your successes to the next level and give you the abundance in it. How does your business glorify God? It glorifies Him by serving God's people. The way we do it God's way is to give our talents, treasure, time, and resources to heaven so that our abundance can flow.

Our creator is so amazing that He wants us to live in the fullness of His blessings. He anoints our head with oil and our cups runneth over. (Psalms 23:3 KJV)

When we do it God's way, He will give us more than enough. The Bible tells us in Ephesians 3: 20-21 (NIV), now to Him who is able to do immeasurably more than all we ask or imagine, according to His power that is at work within us, to Him be glory in the church and in Christ Jesus throughout all generations, for ever and ever! Amen.

What you do now with your business and ministry today is for your legacies to come.

If God can create creation in six days, surely it won't take long for him to create your business if you just turn it to the Creator.

If we do the natural business that He gave us, do it His Way, and put Super (God's power) on it, God will take the natural business and do the supernatural with it.

Let us ALWAYS do our business God's Way!

Prayer

Dear Heavenly Father, I exalt you, I love you and I adore you. I bless your Holy name for you are Holy. You are Awesome and Glorious in all your ways. You know all and you see all. I come before you with a grateful and a thankful heart. I am humbled that you chose me. I thank you for trusting me with every ministry, every business, every opportunity so that I can bless your children with my God given gifts and talents, so that you may be glorified. So today God I confess that everything I have and everything I own belongs to you. I turn my businesses and ministry over to you. I trust you to do whatever you want to with my businesses. I know that your way is far greater than mine. You will always lead me to the expected end. I know your ways are not our ways and that your results will accomplish the task that you set before me. Isaiah 55:8-9 says, "For my thoughts are not your thoughts, nor are your ways my ways," says the Lord. For as the heavens are higher than the earth, so are my ways higher than your ways, and my thoughts than your thoughts. Although the world may contradict your ways, I am deliberate in living out your will over my life and businesses. I decree and declare that my businesses are successful and that they become a blessing to your people. I bind every demon, every imp that comes against the assignments that you have entrusted me with. I declare that I possess the confidence and resilience to manage these assignments. No weapon formed against me shall prosper and every tongue that rise up against me shall be condemned. I decree and declare that success is my portion. Impart your wisdom in me that I may do what is right, what is good, what is just and what is pure. I thank you for my successful businesses, I know that every good and perfect gift comes from you. And I thank you for the wealth that you've given me the ability to produce and the streams in dry places in the Matchless Name of Jesus. Amen.

Puzzle Pieces of the Fruit of the Spirit

Dr. Roz Knighten-Warfield

Galatians 5:22-26 (NLT)

I love puzzles! Not a day goes by when I don't use puzzle pieces as a metaphor for how God created us as spirit, mind, and body. Be still and know that I am God is a scripture that comes to mind. Being still, I was reminded about Paul's life. Paul, I'd say, was a reformist. His name was changed from Saul to Paul. A man who once killed Christians was teaching and writing many love stories to teach the people about Jesus Christ, the Son of God. The God who transformed Paul and forgave him for all the killings he had done. God forgives our sins and teaches us to forgive ourselves.

I imagine a puzzle box top cover with Paul teaching the people of Galatia. Can you imagine it with me? Paul in a dark, dreary, wet, cold prison, by candlelight, writing love letters about how he loved and appreciated the people of Galatia. This letter of hope transitioned into six chapters teaching the difference between those who believe and those who did not believe.

Paul shared the toxic fruit in Galatians 5:19-21. To name some of these challenged acts, strife, hatred, selfish ambitions, idolatry, sorcery, envy, and much more. Thank you Lord, oh my soul for the fruit of the Spirit, those being, love, joy, peace, patience, kindness, goodness, faithfulness, gentleness, and self-control. Interesting like two bookends—you see love on one end and self-control on another and wedged between the two are seven other attributes. These nine attributes teach how to emulate Christ. There's no excuse about how to act at home, in the public and even serving your customers in your faith-based business.

Love seeks the highest good in others. Joy is happiness not based on life circumstances. Peace is contentment with self and others. Patience is not being anxious and being slow to speak and slow to anger. Kindness is His mercies are new each day. Goodness is being open, willing, and ready for generosity. Faithfulness is loyalty and being full of trust. Gentleness is living life in a nonthreatening manner. Self-Control is living a life surrendered, obedient, and abiding radically. Remember, these attributes serve as standards to develop characteristics that offer integral means to love self and God's people.

Paul went through a lot of persecution himself; nevertheless, he remained focused on his love for Jesus Christ, the Son of God. Wow, those are some puzzle pieces that all the pieces fit indeed.

Questions:

- What attributes do you need to work on?
- Declare no more residue of the traits that hinder you from walking with God.
- Take a season and study the life of Paul.
- Walk in rhythm with the Fruit of the Spirit.

- Do you know you were saved to serve?

Now, how will you make this look like you? Search out a foundational scripture and study and understand the text. As you repeat the study ask God what assignments, He has for you and be amazed of the newness that will blossom from your 1/1 time with Daddy.

Prayer

Daddy, thank you for Paul's experiences. I feel free that I'm not the only one who has done badly, but now I take up the mantle and evangelize all about King Jesus who died on the cross for me and rose on the third day. This is what I call love. Daddy, thank you for loving me unconditionally. In Jesus name. Amen!

#PuzzlePieces4Life

Let Grace Abound

Anitra Truelove

And God is able to make all grace [every favor and earthly blessing] come in abundance to you, so that you may always [under all circumstances, regardless of the need] have complete sufficiency in everything [being completely self-sufficient in Him] and have an abundance for every good work and act of charity.

2 Corinthians 9:8 AMP

My father named me Anitra, which means "grace". Understanding that the father brings identity, I was honored to walk in the definition of what my father named me. People noticed that there was an "essence" that I carried and that I did things in excellence no matter whom I was serving or what role I was operating in. People then started nicknaming me "Anitraness", serving others in excellence through grace. I learned that honor goes a long way. When I was assigned to a difficult person or task, I always understood the power of honoring the position, even if the person was difficult.

I also received a blueprint from my spiritual father, Cesar Nieto, for my call to reform nations. The blueprint offers steps that will give you a divine perspective for handling challenging situations, employees, bosses, customers and even help you to address generational strongholds in your bloodline. If these steps are applied, it will cause you to experience a manifestation of breakthrough. It starts with the meaning of my name, "grace". First, grace connects you to favor, which brings you to honor, it leads you to a divine perspective (God's perspective), which causes you to have a renewed mind. Lastly, once your mind is renewed you then can reform nations. When handling any situation, it is important to learn to extend grace to those that seem undeserving, and it positions favor to be released in your life. In addition, learning how to approach any circumstance in honor will reveal a divine perspective which is God's view of what he sees. Once you have God's revelation it will cause your mind to be renewed. You cannot address behavior without addressing the culture. Understanding the why behind someone's culture will also give you clarity on how to approach a circumstance. Once your mind is renewed then reformation takes place. I have found such beauty in being graceful and watching walls drop through honoring. All the steps lead to reforming nations. Following these steps are not always easy, but if you are intentional about putting them into practice, I Decree, you will start experiencing breakthrough. The more you experience breakthrough grace will abound, and miracles will be your new mindset.

Submit yourselves to [the authority of] every human institution for the sake of the Lord [to honor His name], whether it is to a king as one in a position of power, or to governors as sent by him to bring punishment to those who do wrong, and to praise and encourage those who do right. For it is the will of God that by doing right you may silence (muzzle, gag) the [culpable] ignorance and irresponsible criticism of foolish people. Live as free people, but do not use your freedom as a cover or pretext for evil, but [use it and live] as bond-servants of God. Show respect for all people [treat them honorably], love the brotherhood [of believers], fear God, honor the King. 1 Peter 2:13-17 AMP

Prayer

Father God, I thank you that you named me, that you can give me a blueprint that lines up with my name, my call, my mandate, and my business. I thank you for giving me the strength to serve with grace when those that you called me to are difficult to work with or even love. Help me to honor the position even when a person needs deliverance or my expertise. Father, thank you for giving me the ability to have a divine perspective of my family, business, and mission when I feel overwhelmed. I know my help comes from you, the maker of heaven and earth. I declare and decree, Romans 8:18, for I consider [from the standpoint of faith] that the sufferings of the present life are not worthy to be compared with the glory that is about to be revealed to us and in us! God, I thank you that I serve others as if I am serving you. Examine my heart and expose anything that is not pleasing to you that would hinder my progression. Allow me to extend grace to myself for change and love unconditionally. I thank you that I walk in the grace that connects me to favor, that leads me to honor. I pray people will be blessed by my essence and reformed by your name, in Jesus' name. Amen!

Living for
His Purpose

Dr. Janine Graham-Howard

*For I know the plans I have for you, declares the Lord, plans to prosper you
and not to harm you, plans to give you hope and a future.*
Jeremiah 29:11 (NIV)

The Lord impregnated me with purpose, and I gave birth to this ministry called Living for His Purpose Women's Ministry. The vision of the ministry is to encourage every woman of God to live according to the purpose that God has created for YOU. It would be a shame if we would live all our lives and never live according to what God has purposed for us to do. Every year I host a conference for Living for His Purpose Women's Ministry. During this conference our goal is for every woman to leave with purpose. With our logo —a butterfly—the theme of every conference is Fly Butterfly Fly.

We all start off as eggs and then go to the Larva stage, the caterpillars, and during different stages in our life, we go through this metamorphosis. During the last stage—the pupa stage—we burst out of the cocoon into beautiful butterflies. It takes some butterflies two weeks to come out, and some all winter, but that butterfly will eventually come out. This is the same for you. When you come out, you may be a little shaky, but you will FLY.

What phase are you in... egg, larva or the pupa? There is a butterfly in all of us, and the world is ready to see your beauty. Think about what stage you are in with your business endeavors. If you put it in God's hand, surely it will be a beautiful butterfly.

I speak prophetically that God has been trying to break through the cocoon that you or your business has been hiding in, but in fifteen (15) days, God says SHONDO, the Greek word, for "He's turning things around for you". You will live on purpose, and your business and your ministry will live on purpose. The Bible says in, Jeremiah 29:11, I know the plans that I have for you. God knows why He created you. Why don't we all tune into that very thing that God has impregnated us with to glorify His Kingdom? You know you were created to please Him. Every day you wake up, wake up with purpose.

Know where you are going and go on purpose.

Know what you are doing and do it on purpose.

Start that business on purpose.

Know what you are going to say and speak on purpose.

Know what you are praying and pray on purpose.

Know that you have been purposefully made.

Prayer

Heavenly Father thank you for purposing my life before I ever had a plan for myself. I know that your plans will never fail me, but they will prevail. God, you cause all things to happen at exactly the right time! Trusting you brings my purpose all together. I don't have to try to figure it out when I know

I have you leading and guiding me in every way. I am not going to give up or give in. I am holding on to the purpose in my life. I know you want the best for me and through my preparation will come elevation. I know you will promote me if I continue to do the right thing. Your grace is sufficient. So, God, I know you will never send me into a situation alone; you are there leading, guiding and directing. So, as I pursue my purpose God, please lead me to balance my time, energy and resources between fulfilling my purpose for family, career and mostly my relationship with you.

Let me prioritize my life accordingly. Let me be sensitive to your spirit. All things are working for my good. Let me bring glory to you with my purpose. Place me in rooms that I did not inquire about. Open doors that man tried to shut. Sign contracts that they said I could not get on my own. Let my ultimate purpose come forth in the Name of Jesus. As I embrace my purpose today, I accept the reason that you have created me, and I declare from this day forward that I will live for your purpose. In Jesus' Name. Amen.

You Can Defeat the Enemy

Chanel Blackmore

For as he thinks in his heart, so is he.
Proverbs 23:7 (NKJV)

I've been in business longer than I care to admit. My husband and I knew immediately that a nine-to-five job would not be enough for us to support our family. We had three children, two of which were girls who were into cheerleading and dance, as well as a son who was in every sport. Needless to say, we were strapped weekly for cash. At the end of every week, there was always a lack. This situation prompted us to begin a fierce search for a business that could help our family thrive and not just survive.

By the end of the school year, I was so discouraged. We'd tried everything... We'd tried Mary Kay, Specialty Merchandise Corporation (SMC), and other popular MLMs and failed miserably. Not that we weren't selling; it was the ROI (return on investment) that was lacking. The time and energy it took just to make the money wasn't worth it.

One day, when I was in prayer, I heard the Spirit say, "Child, what's in your hand?" It was so clear that I literally looked down at my hands. It made me think, what do I have that I can produce that could make me financially secure? I quickly made a list of everything I knew how to do. At the end, I was so stoked... Until fear crept in. As I reviewed my list, I thought, nobody's going to buy this! Who's going to pay ME to do these things? I don't have a degree; I only have my medical background. Who I am right now isn't enough... These thoughts kept me bound not only in my head, but they kept me from executing. You see, 90% of spiritual warfare occurs in the mind. The enemy battles with us there. It's where he goes when he wants to sow doubt and fear. It's his favorite place to plant seeds of failure and strife.

I want to explain something here. Thoughts are energy. We can feel negative energy just like positive energy. The Word says that as a man thinketh, so is he. Simply stated, this means you are what you think. Our thoughts shape us and inspire us to take action. There will be many people in your life who are truly supportive and then there are those who are not. I want to warn you to look inward for support. The Lord has given you all you need to get to the next level!

Listen, the enemy never wants you to achieve your goals. He doesn't want you to bless the masses with your gifts; he wants you to be afraid to show the world what you can do. He doesn't want you helping people get free from bondage; he wants you to over think and over analyze everything. These are all signs of procrastination. Fear can manifest in many different ways. Fear can manifest as:

- Doubt
- Frustration
- Anxiety

- Poverty

Sometimes you can feel things one way and they stem from something totally different. Always think about these things and really discern where they come from. Our thoughts have tremendous power. One thought can affect your entire day.

For example, you can start out at one moment, feeling really empowered, and one thought can take you in an entirely different direction. The enemy will use your thoughts to influence your life. Take, for instance, you get up in the morning and stub your toe. Immediately you can think (thought), this is going to be a bad day! Then you walk around getting ready and you feel anxious. All the while, the thought of a "bad day" looming in the back of your mind. Once you get into your car, the traffic is horrible and there it is again (thought). Now you're in a horrible mood and everyone SEES it (behavior/actions). At the end of the day, nothing goes your way, so you confirm what you initially thought; you had a bad day.

You see, it's a vicious cycle! Imagine if we did what the Word says about our thought life!

Finally, brethren, whatsoever things are true, whatsoever things are honest, whatsoever things are just, whatsoever things are pure, whatsoever things are lovely, whatsoever things are of good report; if there be any virtue, and if there be any praise, think on these things. Philippians 4: 8 (KJV)

When I first started my coaching practice, my first thought was about what my family would think. What would others say about me, especially the ones who knew about my past? The enemy will have you caught up in your head thinking of things that no one else is thinking. You must push through those thoughts! Remember who you are! You are a child of the Most High God! You were born to walk in favor and excellence. Every time you pray, you remember that everything with our Father is YES and AMEN! These are the thoughts you want to reside in your head. These are the things you must think about! What does the Word say about you? It says that you CAN'T lose! You were created in the image of an all-powerful God. How can you fail? God created you for victory!

Prayer

Dear Abba Father,

Thank you for giving me the key to keeping my thoughts in line with your word. Understanding that the mind is the battleground of my enemy helps me know how to fight! I will always remember that I have the mind of Christ and in doing so, I will never allow the enemy to take control of my thoughts. I will guard my thought life with vigilance and care. I will arrest every thought that exalts itself against your word.

I will replace thoughts with scripture and remember that I am the head and NOT the tail! I am victorious because of the blood of Christ! Amen!

Purpose

Keisa Campbell

Before I formed you in the womb I knew you, before you were born I set you apart; I appointed you as a prophet to the nations.
Jeremiah 1:5 (NIV)

On the journey to living a fulfilled life, you will encounter some ups and some downs in every area of your life. I like to refer to "living a fulfilled life" as Beautiful Living®. But before I go any further, let me take a moment to tell you what Beautiful Living is. Beautiful Living is whole-life wellness. It is living and operating in purpose, and, in turn, living a life of fulfillment in every area of your life. Founded on seven pillars, Beautiful Living focuses on mental, spiritual, physical, relational, financial, career, and outward beauty.

When I speak of Beautiful Living, I'm ultimately insisting that you identify what your purpose is so that you may live a life of abundance. But know that Beautiful Living will look different for everyone and that you are the only person who can define what Beautiful Living looks like for you, and that starts with knowing your purpose.

Purpose (noun) – the reason for which something is done or created or for which something exists.

I'm sure that you have heard how important purpose is, or maybe you are on your purpose journey. Or perhaps you have even been asked, "Do you know what your purpose is?" Maybe only one or all applies to you but know that each of us were born with a purpose and a calling that you can either discover or completely miss.

Often, you operate out of purpose because of what's going on in your world, (i.e., being a mother, a wife, the work that you do, or even life's trauma) and you miss the ultimate calling on your life because you get stuck in the responsibilities that come with those titles, the unfulfilling work that you are doing to make ends meet, or even the trauma that makes you feel like your world is ending. Not to say that being a mother or wife is not a purpose, because it is. I became a teen mom at 14. My daughter became my purpose to make sure that I graduated so that I could take care of her. But, within that purpose, I discovered my purpose while in high school, which I had been doing since the age of eight. I was constantly in situations where I had to encourage and uplift others and not just my peers, but my teachers as well. Then, I became a wife at 21, and found myself still encouraging, uplifting, guiding, and coaching others. I later divorced at 40 and was still being called to encourage, uplift, guide, and coach others amid what I was going through.

Purpose doesn't change because of life circumstances… the only thing that may change is who you serve and how you serve them. So, besides the titles that I have held and life circumstances, I have always been called to encourage, uplift, guide, and coach others outside of my household.

So what work is God calling you to do? Who is He calling you to serve outside of your household? Does the work that you do have an impact on others, and do you feel fulfilled during and after doing the work? Or are you left feeling miserable? Your purpose in life answers a simple question: How is someone's life better because they crossed your path?

Knowing and operating in your purpose is essential. Purpose gives you a reason to get up in the morning. Purpose allows you to know what goals to set, it also gives you a sense of direction. When you are operating in purpose, it helps to guide your life decisions and create meaning for life. Your purpose should give you a sense of fulfillment. Your purpose is important because it allows you to look beyond yourself and your own needs to a bigger picture. Your purpose is to help and serve others. So, whatever your purpose, it should serve and help others.

Scripture says that before God formed you in your mother's womb, He knew you and it goes on to say that God set you apart before you were born and appointed you a prophet to the nations (Jeremiah 1:5 NIV). He created you on purpose with a purpose. Jeremiah 29:11 NIV, tells us He already knows the plans that he has for your life. Those plans are to prosper you and not to harm you, plans to give you hope and a future.

Purpose drives your mindset, your relationship with God, how you take care of your body, and the relationship that you have with yourself, as well as the relationship that you have with others. It drives your finances and whether you take the career path, entrepreneurship path, or do a hybrid. Purpose also determines how you show up for what you have been called to do. When you have a sense of purpose, you experience less loneliness and make better lifestyle choices that ultimately benefit your health. All in all, knowing your purpose is your life compass.

So, the question is, are you living and operating in your purpose? Do you feel a sense of fulfillment when you wake up every day? Are you making an impact in the world? Or are you on a constant hamster wheel trying to figure out what God is calling you to do? Operating in purpose allows you to live a beautiful life.

Affirmation
I am fulfilled in every area of my life. My mindset is beautiful, my relationship with God is beautiful, and I love my body and treat it well, knowing that it's the only temple that I have. I am cultivating healthy relationships. I am the lender and not the borrower... my finances are being multiplied. I am operating in my purpose and showing up for who God has called me to be. When I walk into any space, I command it because I walk with authority, and I'm dressed for the part. Beautiful Living is my birthright, and I am making an impact in the world.

Prayer
God, I thank you for life. Thank you for the assignment that you have given me. Ephesians 2:10 NIV says that I am your handiwork, created in Jesus Christ to do good works, which you prepared in advance for me to do. God, you have created me for a purpose, to do good works, tailor-made just for me. God, I give you, my yes. Yes, to the assignment that you have assigned to my life. Yes, to the people that you have attached to my assignment. I ask that you order my steps today. That I fulfill every purpose that you created for me to fulfill on this day. I ask that you give me a fresh vision for your purpose

for my life… that my eyes, ears, heart, and mind are opened and in alignment with you so that I may live out my purpose. Father God, I ask that you remove anything that will hinder me from living and operating in your will for my life and discerning your vision. Draw me closer to you so that I may discern your voice and be focused on your divine vision for my life. I thank you that even though I have my own ideas of how my life should look, your ultimate purpose prevails. Please align my ideas with yours for your ways are higher than mine and your plans are greater than mine, and nothing is impossible with you. Lead me every step of the way. Lord, I thank you. In Jesus' name. Amen.

Beautiful Living Awaits…

The Revolution of Revelation

Pretina Lowery

But as it is written: Eye has not seen, nor ear heard, nor have entered into the heart of man the things which God has prepared for those who love Him.
1 Corinthians 2:9 (NKJV)

Have you ever lain awake at night until your eyes looked like peppermints? Asking why did this relationship fail? Wondering why wasn't I chosen for that position, or why does it seem like everyone around me but me is walking in the favor of God? Of course, you have because I have too. You decide to reach out to a friend, expecting them to know why things are happening or are not happening to you or for you. You may even attend church hoping the Pastor would say something that resonates with you; only for the sermon topic to be on tithing. All the while, your best option is to stop and ask the God of Glory to divulge what is actually occurring. He alone desires to reveal to us facts and favor amid fog and friction. He gives supernatural sight to see beyond our circumstances, ears to hear His voice, and fills our hearts with the desire-to-desire what He wants for us.

In doing so, it always turns out to be much more than we could have ever imagined.

Will you ask him to reveal what's been concealed?

Prayer

Eternal God, our father, I know that all wisdom comes from you. When I lack wisdom, you have given me a gracious invitation to ask and receive your insight on how to navigate through this gift called life. Human wisdom profits nothing compared to your unlimited knowledge, so I look to the invisible God alone to bring clarity and creativity. You alone bless the works of my hands and cause me to gain wealth. I pray and believe you for divine interactions, an abundance of new clientele and the return of former contracts. May my hands be clean and heart pure as I humbly govern and steward what you have placed in my care. I thank you for every transaction, phone call, meeting, and networking opportunity. Whatever understanding I acquired thus far, I ask that you breathe on it and resurrect any areas that need revision. Place my name on the hearts and in the heads of billionaires. Grant me access to not only be in rooms of expansion but also the power and authority to become those who will plan strategies and spaces that make room for up-and-coming entrepreneurs. May integrity go before me, and balanced scales be my rear guard. May the eyes of my understanding be enlightened that I will see each person as a reflection of your grace and formation. May I serve them with compassion, patience, and excellence. I ask these things in congruence with the name of Christ. Amen.

God's Way is Sweet

Dr. Janine Graham-Howard

How sweet are thy words unto my taste! yea, sweeter than honey to my mouth!

Psalms 119:103 KJV

I used to have the worst sweet tooth! Growing up, I never cared much about eating sweets, but as I became an adult and my pallet changed, sweets were at the top of my list. I wasn't concerned about it being healthy for me—it was my enjoyable pleasure. Restaurants with the better dessert menu? That's where I dined. My love for desserts caused me to become very interested in making the desserts that I loved to eat so much. I worked diligently, learning to bake and make candies. No, I never went to culinary school, but I became an awesome home baker! To learn even more, I read cookbooks, watched videos, went to the mothers of the church, gathered all the knowledge I could, and started making desserts. Instead of me and my family always indulging in these desserts by ourselves, I would put them in sample boxes and take them to my job at the hospital, so that my co-workers could enjoy them as well. The nurses, doctors and staff always wanted more. My guilty pleasure became a side hustle.

Many times, giving away my samples turned into sales. I started Neen's Treats.

Pound cake, red velvet cake, German chocolate cake, cheese-cake brownies, milk chocolate fudge, peanut butter fudge, million-dollar pies, sweet potato pies, sweet potato cheesecake bread pudding with sauce, peach cobbler, apple pie, peanut brittle, pecan pie, butter cookies, peanut butter cookies, oatmeal raisin cookies and homemade candies. I made them all.

Oh, how sweet it is!

These are some sweets that grace my family's table and that I still love to make. Some of these desserts are easier to make than others, but they have the same outcome of being a sweet delight.

When it comes to the things of God, there are some things that are easier to do than others, but they all have the same outcome.

Hard work God's way has sweet outcomes.

But there is something sweeter and will enlighten your taste buds like nothing else.

It is so sweet that it will satisfy any craving you have.

So sweet that it will wake you out of your sleep desiring more.

So sweet that it will be the most nutritional meal you have ever had.

Oh, how sweet it is… the Word of God.

As we continue to work the works that God has so prepared for us, let us continue to sup on the sweetness of God's Word as He directs every business, ministry, and entrepreneurial adventure that we embark upon. Some may come to us by accident, like Neen's treats.

Don't just satisfy your sweet tooth with sweets, satisfy it with the sweet knowledge of the Word of God. Let Him lead, guide, and direct you as God anoints to sign contracts and supernaturally puts you in places to make deals. He's deliciously great.

Prayer

Dear Heavenly Father, how sweet are your words. The Bible says they are sweeter than honey to my mouth. As the Creator of the heavens and the earth and all living things, God you know what's best for me. I know that your Word is not only sweet, but nourishing. I thank you for allowing your Word to be nourishment to my soul. As I take on every guided adventure that you have unctioned me to do, let me eat the meat of your Word as I work toward my goals. Let me continue to do my best no matter hard it may seem or how difficult it may get. Let my words and my speech be gracious to those that cross my path. Kindness shall go a long way in my business. After people meet me, let them see you and desire to know you or even want more of you. As I cultivate my appetite toward you and your Word, let me experience the fullness of the sweetness of your Word. I will taste and see that you are good. Let me greet those that you send me with a compassionate heart. I know your outcome is ALWAYS SWEET! I thank you in advance, and I give you glory over my life and business adventures in the Mighty Name of Jesus. Amen.

Devil, You Better Watch Your Mouth!

Chanel Blackmore

No weapon that is formed against you shall prosper, and every tongue that shall rise against you in judgement you shall condemn. This is the heritage of servants of God, and their righteousness is of me, says the Most High God.
Isaiah 54:17 (KJV)

One thing you will face in business is people who don't support you. There are those who have been watching you from the onset of your entrepreneurial journey and many wish you well. However, there are some who are waiting to see you fail. You must put on the whole armor of the Lord when you're out here working in the Kingdom. If it was easy, everyone would do it. Kingdom work is rife with obstacles and challenges. The thing you must remember is that God has your back!

Here's what the scripture says:

"No weapon that is formed against you shall prosper."

Wow! He didn't say that the weapon wouldn't be formed. I know that's against everything that we've been taught in the past but listen; He says that the weapon won't prosper. What does that mean? It means that though 100 enemies may encamp around you and shoot a thousand arrows, but not one will strike you. Simply put, it means that you're untouchable! It means that 10,000 people can write about you in a nasty post about you or your business on social media, but 50,000 will come to your defense. It means that folks can spread lies about you and one person will come forth and declare your innocence and your business integrity. You see, the weapon was formed, but it didn't prosper!

"So they shall fear the name of the Lord from the West, and His glory from the rising of the sun. When the enemy shall come in like a flood, the Spirit of the LORD shall lift a standard against him." Isaiah 59:19 (KJV)

This scripture always makes me laugh. It says that everyone from the west to the east shall fear Him…. Come on now! EVERYONE. Who is the "everyone" in your life? Who's coming in like a flood to destroy your good name? Who's coming against you, praying that you fail? The Word clearly says that He (God) will lift up a standard against them! This means that He will make an example out of them! This should have made some of you stop and give Him praise! There is no weapon that can destroy what He's blessed and ordained!

Now let's get to my favorite part of the scripture. Look at what it says:

"and every tongue that shall rise against you in judgement you shall condemn".

It says that when the enemy takes control of someone's tongue to spew hatred, that YOU shall condemn them! Now that's powerful! That means that you, through prayer, will make them eat their words! How? By moving forward in your gift. By blessing others. By standing firm in the space that God created for you. This is how you win!

I remember a time when a co-worker was constantly making trouble for me. You see, we were both up for the same promotion. When I received the promotion and she didn't, she tried to turn my staff against me. I went into prayer immediately. Let me tell you something. When the enemy raises his head against you, go straight into prayer! You don't need to wait to see what he's going to do or where he's going to strike! That's a major mistake we make. We wait to see and by the time we understand what's happening, he's got a stronghold in our lives.

Well, I prayed Psalms 91 daily, petitioning the Lord to move on my behalf. Not some days later, she came to me and asked me for forgiveness. She'd heard how I was fighting for the staff to have more benefits, and she realized she was fighting against an answered prayer.

Y'all, the Lord doesn't play! He shows up when we ask. The point of this is to go into warfare immediately. Don't wait for the enemy to make your life a battlefield or wreak havoc in your business. Sometimes, it's as simple as a whispered prayer. Other times, it's a full-on laying prostrate affair. Either way, you have the victory!

Prayer

Abba Father,

Thank you for always having my back. Your Word says that you will close the mouth of my enemies. I'm grateful to be reminded that I am protected by your Spirit. NOTHING the enemy has planned for me will work. Thank you for planting me in the Kingdom to do your will according to the gifting of the Spirit. Help me remember that I am yours and you are mine; that everything I'm doing, you've called me to do it. Therefore, I am divinely equipped to move in the spaces of the enemy unscathed. And Father, I will always remember that during the times of attack, I will run into prayer immediately. In Jesus' name. Amen.

Matters of the Heart

Kelina Morgan

As water reflects the face, so one's life reflects the heart.
Proverbs 27:19 (NIV)

Women, our hearts should be a space where we honor God. A place of true worship; not just lip worship. Our hearts, in our obedient worship to God, lead us to righteousness and right decisions. It is important that we guard what enters our hearts as, out of the abundance of the heart, the mouth speaks. As a woman thinks, so she is, and our heart reflects who we are. We guard our hearts by guarding our thought life; what we think on and allow to enter our thoughts, what we give space for, is what shall be. We must discern and have wisdom. As a woman in business, it is important that what we give our time and space to in our thoughts produces, builds, elevates, grows, empowers, and builds wealth for God's kingdom.

There are so many books on the mindset and characteristics of an entrepreneur, which means there are some mindsets and characteristics that are not that of an entrepreneur as well. There are things that have no place in the mind of an entrepreneur. We are builders and those things that block, tear down, or erode what we are building have no place in our hearts. So, we are going to pray against those things, and pray for the things that help us build and grow, personally and in business:

Prayer

Father, in the matchless name of Jesus, I come before you. I ask you:

- *Watch over and purify my heart.*
- *Help me to replace old, bad habits with new and better ones; ones that support the visions you have given me.*
- *I know that every arena of my life intersects with what's going on in my heart.*
- *I ask that you let me not defile my efforts by the words I speak from my heart, but prompt and compel me to speak that which strengthens, builds, and grows my efforts.*
- *Let me not think evil thoughts against anyone, especially any other woman and business owner. Instead, let me think positively, affirming thoughts of support for fellow women and business owners to build alliances and community.*
- *Heal me of all wounds—loss, rejection, or disappointment.*
- *Help me trust you and have faith in you even when I have not seen it.*
- *Help me build trust in others who are there to support me and my business. Give me discernment in this area.*
- *Remind me to pray and fast for my business, families, and other women entrepreneurs.*
- *Father, forgive me for feeling hindered by guilt or shame or thoughts that I did something wrong or made a mistake. I confess it and I*

release in the name of Jesus! I have no debt. Jesus paid it all and covered it. I now know better, and I do better.

- *I let go of hurt, anger, and disappointment. I release the people that hurt me and the anger I hold towards them. I release them from the debt. I let all bitterness, anger, wrath, shouting, and slander be removed from me, along with malice. They have no place in me and I hold no space for them anymore.*

- *Father, let me not grow or cultivate the seed of greed in my heart. Let me realize my life is not the sum of what I own, but instead let me be generous in my gifts, wisdom, talents, and even my monetary resources. I am blessed to be a blessing. I endured to help someone else through it. Let me give from my overflow as you saw fit to give it to me without sparing.*

- *Father, you are no respecter of man. What you give to one, you can give to another. There is no good thing you will withhold from those who love you. Let me not covet what others have and ask You Father for what is best for me and what you desire for me. Bless me oh Lord and enlarge my territory, according to your will for my life and business. Let me ask all things with the proper motives that I may receive of you. Let me be a woman and entrepreneur who truly celebrate others, knowing that it takes nothing from me for what you have for me is for me. I lack no good thing, for you give me everything that pertains to life and Godliness. My cups run over and overflow.*

- *Thank you for the witty ideas and inventions that you have and will continue to download in me. Thank you for entrusting me to do your will and be a part of your plan. Thank you for having set me in the marketplace as a beacon of your light. Help me to remember to always represent you as I am an ambassador for Christ.*

- *Father, I know that I have you to rely on and trust in. I can rest in you. You are my strength. Help me not to grow weary in well doing, so that I shall reap. Help me not to faint. Strengthen me. Father, I thank you for praying women who are also brilliant, intelligent, talented entrepreneurs who collaborate with me. I give my gifts and talents to you to use as you see fit. I give you all the glory and honor. In Jesus' name I pray. Amen.*

Scripture Reference: John 4:23, Colossians 3:23, Proverbs 14:33, Matthew 15:18, proverbs 16:23, Luke 6:45, Ecclesiastes 10:2, Ephesians 4:34

BODY

Say Yes to Self-Care

Ronisa Glass

And he said to them, "Come away by yourselves to a desolate place and rest a while." For many were coming and going, and they had no leisure even to eat.

Mark 6:31(KJV)

Self-care is defined as the practice of taking action to preserve or improve one's own health; the practice of taking an active role in protecting one's own well-being and happiness, in particular during periods of stress. So, let's take a hard dive into the reasons why we need self-care. When we mesh things together between life (that's happening all around us, family that's always pulling on us, friends who often need us and work, "daily occupation for some") and your business—which is the very thing we were called to do—we often forget to stop filling up our basket. The moment we go to pick it up, we realize it's much heavier than we thought it would be. Not anymore! Self-care isn't just good for you, it's good for your productivity. Write your self-care activities on a few post-it notes and strategically place them around your area as a constant reminder to not take on too much. It will help avoid things such as insomnia, restlessness, fatigue, upset stomach, muscle tension, irritability, social withdrawal, substance abuse, and a lack of motivation. Point to yourself and say, "Self-care means I care about myself!

Prayer

Father, in the Name of Jesus, I come to You right now, oh God, first thanking you for this time of inward reflection. I rest in this moment, allowing you to turn my worry away about my own self-care. I get it now, oh God. Self-care means I care, and I care about myself. I lift my hands to receive your blessings today. I pray you will continue to anoint me with strength and self-care. Father, I thank you that this is not just for today, but it's for tomorrow and it's always. Lord, I pray in the name of Jesus that you will grant grace to me. Let me be motivated and inspired to accept your hand working diligently in my life. Lord, I pray for more patience within me and for more wisdom. Not only in business, but how to take care of myself. So, Father, I pray right now that you will continue to encourage me throughout the day to take the correct steps to walk proudly and upright and to behave well. I know I am a representative of you. Help me master each lesson. I thank you for everything in Jesus' name! Thank You for continuing to touch my business. I want to not only pursue everything you called me to do, but I want to do it with intentionality. I not only will take care of myself, but I will do so mentally. Lord, help me stabilize my mind. I will also take care of myself spiritually. Help me to continue having a one-on-one relationship with you and doing so in the intimacy that you so desire when I pray, praise, worship and wait on you. I want to be a good steward of that which you've given me, so I ask you to help me get better at managing my money so that my personal life and my business can be sustained. It is my heart's desire to have wealth for Kingdom business. Help me Lord, to be emotionally healthy so that I am not tossed to and fro by the things of life and circumstances around me. Help me with self-care physically oh God. Help me to discard and put off anything that may try to attach itself to me physically, in an attempt to hold me bound. I pray in the Name of Jesus, that you will block it oh God. I not only plead the blood of Jesus over myself, but over every single businesswoman and entrepreneur. I thank you in advance for the elevation in business in this season. I believe you're going to blow my mind. As I attend to "self" through obedience to your Word, I know you will attend to me. I thank you Lord, and I bless you because I truly believe in self-care now. I will take the intentional time to breathe Lord. I will be intentional about taking time to refocus and realign. I won't lose sight of the very thing that you called me to do oh God. I thank You for strategically choosing me for it. I will be diligent and obedient about my self-care, purpose, and your plan oh God. I bless you on this day! In Jesus matchless name I pray. Amen!

Getting Dressed/Styled Spiritually for Entrepreneurs

Blessing Shuman

Therefore, as God's chosen people, holy and dearly loved, clothe yourselves with compassion, kindness, humility, gentleness and patience.
Colossians 3:12 (NIV)

When you think about wardrobe styling, what usually comes to mind? For many, it may include a perfect, figure-accenting outfit, paired with the perfect pair of shoes, and sealed with the perfect accessories. With the boost of confidence that usually comes when we know or feel like we look good, we can then walk boldly into every room anticipating a show-stopping entrance.

Entrepreneurs spend thousands of dollars with curated style boards and new clothing just to enjoy temporary confidence. I have had the pleasure of serving many clients who have done the same, only to later express insecurity if the meeting didn't go as planned. With this in mind, what if I told you that the most important "styling" that's necessary for us not only as entrepreneurs, but as women of faith, has nothing to do with the material and all to do with the spiritual?

In Colossians 3:12 NIV, Paul encourages us with "Therefore, as God's chosen people, holy and dearly loved, clothe yourselves with compassion, kindness, humility, gentleness and patience." No matter what you wear on the outside, it's what we put on by the help of the Holy Spirit inwardly that will allow us to truly shine to the glory of God as entrepreneurs. While we can have on the most expensive outfit as we enter a board meeting, sharing the compassion and kindness of God is what will allow doors to open that will leave us in awe. We can pay a personal stylist to purchase a whole new wardrobe for us as we endeavor in our businesses, but it's the humility, gentleness, and patience of God that will allow us to trust Him for the increase we are believing for in our businesses.

When I started my career as a personal stylist, I never wanted to style women in outfits as a coverup for their brokenness. Only after a moment of encouragement and healing, it is always such a joy to adorn my clients with garments that accent their God-given inner beauty.

Sometimes we spend so much time getting prepared to get dressed. However, it is even more important for us to get in God's presence, allowing Him to daily download His character within us, which would allow us to shine as the light of the world (Matt.5: 14-16) through our business and more. To my dear sister—my fellow woman entrepreneur—who is reading this book, who may have the best wardrobe but still wondering what's missing, I encourage you to take a moment and pray with me below. I can only imagine the testimony that will follow.

Prayer

Father in the mighty name of Jesus, thank you for being God, my daddy, my friend, my business partner and the most amazing, necessary Wardrobe Consultant. Father, I thank you. I cannot only seek you to coordinate my outward clothing, but you have given me blood-bought access to your presence, allowing me to coordinate with you concerning everything I need to be clothed with in the Spirit. Through the power of Holy Spirit, I pray for you to clothe me with compassion, kindness, humility, gentleness, and patience according to Colossians 3, verse 12. As I get dressed in the Spirit realm daily, I pray for the fruit of your borrowed light to shine through me in every atmosphere you grace me to enter. May the prosperity of my business and the influence of your character through me bring glory to your name all the days of my life. It is in Jesus' name I pray. Amen.

When the Entrepreneur is the Caregiver

Angela McGowan

I can do all things [which He has called me to do] through Him who strengthens and empowers me [to fulfill His purpose—I am self-sufficient in Christ's sufficiency; I am ready for anything and equal to anything through Him who infuses me with inner strength and confident peace.]
Philippians 4:13 (AMP)

W hen you're the caregiver! Regardless of whether you were appointed, nominated, or volunteered as a caregiver, you begin the task willingly but definitely unprepared for the full assignment!

I can speak about this life directly and without hesitation because I was the caregiver for my husband. I know and remember the caregiving life. Many months of sacrificing, devotion, love, the extreme physical tiredness and the many, many days of sheer emotional exhaustion!

Although there are many healing scriptures that would come to your mind immediately, I would like to share with you a few that will help you the caregiver and the businesswoman that I used, and you can use today and the days ahead.

1. For I know the plans and thoughts that I have for you, "says the Lord; plans for peace and well-being and not disaster, to give you a future and a hope! Jeremiah 29:11 (Message Bible)
2. But thanks be to God who always leads us in triumph in Christ. 2 Corinthians 2:14a (Amplified Bible)
3. I can do all things through Him who strengthens me! Philippians 4:13 (Amplified Bible)

At the beginning of my husband's illness, I had a full-time job, a part-time business, while being a wife, a mother, and a grandmother. But as the days, weeks and months continued; I took a leave from my full-time job to be the primary caregiver. I continued to do my business part time.

I want you to know, understand, and believe that you can give excellent care and you won't miss a beat!

"Why?" you ask. How do I know? Because of the immutable and infallible word of God! When we look at Jeremiah 29:11 it says, "For I know..." Who knows? The Lord. And He says that He's not going to put you in a situation that ends with disaster but will give you a future and a hope!

Second Corinthians 2:14 says to give thanks because it is not sometimes or maybe He will, but it says he always leads us in triumph! Things may not go as fast as you'd like but remember... He says he leads us to triumph. There's your victory right there!

This last verse is your mission statement to recite daily: "I can do all things through Christ who strengthens me."

My sisters, fellow caregivers, and businesswomen... you can do it all and you will not fail!

So, as you read this prayer, read it with belief, read it with faith, and allow it to uplift you, to energize you, to empower you, and to encourage you! Because you can do all things. . . be a wife, a mother, grandmother, a friend, a sister, a businesswoman and most importantly a caregiver with God continuously giving you the strength!

Prayer

Dear God in Jesus name I am asking you to keep me, lead me and guide me during this time of giving care! I realize this special assignment of love is supported 100% by you. I know that I am caring for your child and so I ask you for wisdom in all that I do. I thank you God that every doctor, nurse, or any other medical provider will be used by you anytime care is given during appointments and/or hospitalizations. I ask you to sanctify every pill, every drop of medicine, every needle and IV bag that is introduced to the one that I am giving in care of.

Thank you Lord your blessings flow through me every time I touch the one that you gave me to care for, your child who you love so very much! Father God, I thank you for my business most of all, that you are my business part-ner! I thank you for the vision, the ideas, the step-by-step plan. And so, God because you and I are working together I'm Grateful that even while I am giving care you are opening doors for my business. I thank you because I tithe in this business that you have opened the windows of heaven and are pouring out abundant blessings on my business.

God, I bind the enemy in Jesus' name and every person that wrongfully sows seed of opposition, betrayal, panic, and division in Jesus Name! Lord, thank you for increasing my imagination daily by downloading ideas, concepts, and impressions that will take my business to new heights! Father God thank you Lord for all the customers that you are sending my way because of the bountiful referrals that are created due to the excellent customer service that's given by me and those who work on my team. Today will be a day of great productivity even within small increments of time that I am available! I understand that as I intentionally follow the steps you've ordered in my business you will bless it to overflowing. Lord, I believe your word! 3 John:1 says . . . above all that thou would prosper and be in good health!

Lord, as I am your servant I decree and declare for this caregiving duration with you as my business partner, my business continues to increase in all areas because I am a giver with my time, my talent, and my treasure! God, I know your word never returns void but, it accomplishes that unto which it is sent Isaiah 55:11! I understand, Abundance is my birthright and financial overflow is my legacy! My business continues to expand and receives a hundredfold blessing! Thank you, God! It is done in Jesus' name! Amen.

Beauty From The Inside Out

M'rcedes Jones

I praise you because I am fearfully and wonderfully made; your works are
wonderful, I know that full well.
Psalms 139:14 (NIV)

H ave you ever experienced a time where your hair was done, nails done, dressed to the nines and to everyone else you looked amazing but when you looked in the mirror, you didn't like what you saw? Well, Sis, I'm here to give you a little insight into why that was. You see, beauty comes from within! So often whenever we can't see the beauty on the outside, it's normally because something needs to be healed internally!!!

As a traveling makeup artist, I have met some of the most beautiful women in the world. The one thing that most of them had in common when I first encountered them is that they did not see themselves the way God sees them. From the moment they sat in my chair, they would highlight all the imperfections they wanted me to fix. In reality, the things they wanted to hide were things that made them uniquely them! I want you to read the scripture below and pause to write in your journal what this scripture says to you:

I thank you, God, for making me so mysteriously complex! Everything you do is marvelously breathtaking. It simply amazes me to think about it! How THOROUGHLY you know me, Lord!
Psalms 139:14 (TPT)

We are mysteriously complex, meaning we were not created to be perfect in any way! The imperfections, scars, blemishes, and flaws that we possess are all strategically placed to make us unique; only one of you. There will never be another YOU! Come along with me as we go on a journey to embrace our uniqueness from the inside out.

I've experienced and encountered a lot as an African American woman—in life and in my business. By America's beauty standards, I'm not the ideal person to even be living the life God has allowed me to live. I'm not the thinnest, my skin isn't the lightest and my hair most certainly isn't the straightest. Even in all of that, when I look in the mirror, I am absolutely in love with every part of me I see. It has less to do with my physical features and more to do with what I know pours from the inside out. I don't have a squeaky-clean past, but what I do have is a heart to please God daily and treat ALL His children with love, kindness, and grace.

I grew up in a time where women were ridiculed because of the makeup they wore. Anybody reading this who shies away from doing what they love because of others' opinions, I pray that the spirit of people-pleasing be released from you at this very moment. If you enjoy wearing makeup, Sis, wear the makeup! Gone are the days when we box ourselves in because of what other people may say or think. If it does not contradict who God says you are, then by all means do what makes YOU happy!!!

One year ago, I remember sitting in my car crying because I knew my life was about to change forever due to what God was calling me to birth. I was giving Him all the reasons why He shouldn't use me and, in that moment, I heard ever so clearly, "My experiences make me necessary."

Just as God gave me that revelation about me, I impart it to each and every person that reads this book!

You are necessary.

Your life is necessary.

Your business is necessary.

Your flaws are necessary.

Your imperfections are necessary.

EVERYTHING about YOU is necessary!

And now I want to take this time and pray with you.

Prayer

Father God, I thank you for my life. I thank you even for my flaws and imperfections. I thank you that your Word says in Psalms 139:13-14 (TPT) that you formed my innermost being, shaping my delicate inside and intricate outside, and wove them all together in my mother's womb. God, I thank you for making me so mysteriously complex. Everything you do is marvelously breathtaking. It simply amazes me to think about it. How thoroughly you know me, Lord. And even in knowing the not so good things about me, your love for me is endless. God, I ask that you give me your eyes so that I may see myself just as you see me. I implore the Holy Spirit to come in and show me the areas of my heart that are keeping me from loving myself just as you love me, flaws and all! Father, I thank you for your selfless act of sending your Son to take on my sins when He was a sinless man. Thank you for bestowing upon me a crown of beauty instead of ashes. God, in this moment, I repent for all my sins; the ones that I did knowingly and unknowingly. I thank you for your forgiveness. Thank you for creating me in your image and your likeness. I now have the freedom to see my beauty from the inside out. In your Son Jesus' name. Amen.

Created with a Purpose

Latesha Higgs

For we are God's handwork, created in Christ Jesus to do good works which God prepared in advance for us to do.

Ephesians 2:10 (NIV)

Within the chrysalis of a monarch butterfly, a profound metamorphosis takes place. While in the chrysalis, the old body parts of the caterpillar undergo a truly remarkable and necessary change. When it is time to emerge from the chrysalis and take flight, it is well equipped to carry out its God-given purpose. Like the monarch butterfly and all of God's other wonderful creations, we, too, are created to carry out a purpose. Our purpose answers a question, solves a problem, and advances His Kingdom. As entrepreneurs and leaders, whether it is through the products we sell, or services we provide, God has called each one of us to do a great work (carry out our purpose) to advance His kingdom.

The visions that God has given us as entrepreneurs, CEOs, Executive Directors, or leaders are answers to a question that we were created to solve. While you may benefit from that vision, that benefit wasn't just for you alone. When you think about it, it's quite humbling to know that God created each of us to solve a specific problem on the earth. We are all problem solvers!

Just as God carefully crafted the monarch butterfly in its chrysalis, we must trust Him to prepare and equip us with all we need to carry out the good work He has prepared for us to do. There's no need to worry about how; we only need to go forth and trust His timing, guidance, and wisdom. Don't just trust the process, trust the God of the process. He's doing a good work in you in order for you to do a great work for His Kingdom.

Prayer

Dear Heavenly Father,

You are the ultimate leader and I thank you for sending your Son Jesus Christ to be the ultimate example of an impactful, influential, and effective leader. Lord, I do not take it lightly that you have given me this opportunity for leadership and successful entrepreneurship. Lord, I know fully that leadership and owning a business is a responsibility and not a reward. Therefore, I ask that you divinely impart unto me wisdom, patience, courage, and humility. Show me how to lead with emotional intelligence and Godly love. Lord, let me have the mind of your Son Christ as I facilitate or participate in every meeting. Help and guide me to make the best decisions that I can make based on biblical principles and common sense. Lord, show me how to lead by example. Give me the courage to stand for what is right and true. Let me speak your truth in love. Improve both my communication and listening skills. Grant me favor and success with you and man. Help me stay in the posture of a student. Keep me with a growth-mindset. Enable me to develop fresh innovative ideas to grow and improve the teams, organizations, and people I lead. Show me how to raise the level of productivity of all whom I lead and serve. Help me to plan and execute those plans with precision and effectiveness. Lord, I want to be an impactful, insightful, influential, transformational, and effective leader. Lord, let me face each obstacle and challenge with confidence, courage, and radical faith in you. Lord as a leader exponentially increase my influence, so that I can serve more of your people. Exponentially increase my impact so that through your power, lives will be transformed and exponentially increase my income so that I will give more. Lord, you did it for Abraham, Joseph, Esther, Deborah, and many others, in your word, I humbly ask that you do it for me. Transform me into the transformational leader you have called me to be. Strengthen me to walk confidently and boldly in my anointing, calling, and assignments. Lord, open doors. Direct and guide my footsteps. Make my paths straight. I also ask for protection over my whole being and every vision you have given me. Lord, bless me and make me an answer so that everyone around me will have everything that they need. In Jesus' name, I give thanks and praise for it is already done. Amen.

RELATIONSHIP

Setting Boundaries in Business: Frustration and Familiarity

Brandi Rojas

When Jesus had finished these parables, He left there. And after coming to [Nazareth] His hometown, He began teaching them in their synagogue, and they were astonished, and said, "Where did this Man get this wisdom and these miraculous powers [what is the source of His authority]? Is not this the carpenter's son? Is not His mother called Mary? And are not His brothers, James and Joseph and Simon and Judas? And His sisters, are they not [living here] among us? Where then did this Man get all this [wisdom and power]?" And they took offense at Him [refusing to believe in Him]. But Jesus said to them, "A prophet is not without honor except in his hometown and in his own household." And He did not do many miracles there [in Nazareth] because of their unbelief.
Matthew 13:53-58 (AMP)

W hen we talk about boundaries in business, if you are anything like me, you have a passion for what you do. Nobody forced you into it. You simply possess a passion to see people succeed and thrive! You have a passion to see people expand and grow and the icing on the cake is — you are a Visionary! This means that you already have a scope of what your business can do!

Now I am one who pastors and has a business in my hometown—pray for me! When you are in certain environments—whether it be your hometown, a group or clique—if it's the wrong atmosphere, you stand the risk of only being seen for who you were and not who you are. Sometimes, it's even harder to do business with people that you intimately know, because they may find it difficult to separate the "business" you from the "friend/associate" you. As a result, they may have trouble honoring your vision for your business. There are things that business owners experience with clients who know them outside the business setting, and we, business owners, know they are approaching it that way because it's us! There are some who, despite relationship, will honor you in business—they will pay you when asked and will do everything you say. But then there are those who will attempt to take advantage and have no respect for boundaries. No matter how hard we try, we will always find at least one who will try to break the boundary that has been established.

Before we position ourselves to place blame or begin pointing outward, we must first point inward! At this moment, these become the pivotal questions:

1. Did I enforce the boundary lines?
2. Where did I get frustrated?

In Matthew 7:6 we find these words:

Do not give that which is holy to dogs, and do not throw your pearls before pigs, for they will trample them under their feet, and turn and tear you to pieces."

Now in no way am I calling anyone around you a "pig"—this scripture just shares a simple reality. Truthfully, you can know the worth of a thing, but if you are not careful, you will find yourself presenting your gifts to people who do not appreciate it. When you place something that is deemed precious before an individual who does not appreciate it, you are destined to run into a problem. Likewise, when your mindset has shifted wrong, you can find yourself forcing pearls in wrong places and to the wrong individuals—in other words, making a pure but fatal attempt for one to accept the beauty and potential of what you have in your possession. Sadly, many did not realize just how many do not honor them, until they took a chance to execute vision.

One thing that I have learned as a Pastor, for every person that calls me that in their life, I want to be that for them. Contrary, I also have those who call me Pastor, but have no desire for me to be their Pastor. This truth led me into a place of having to accept the boundary set and building new ones if needed. This is all necessary, especially when we know that the necessity of setting boundaries has the potential to make a business owner bitter. For me, these harsh realities took me captive and nearly swallowed me whole. I no longer desired to go to my office. It felt as if the walls were closing in on me. Literally, frustration took over my anticipation to the point where I did not even trust a client to follow through and would become surprised when they did. I had no desire to read anyone's manuscript. I had no desire to check another email. These types of "hits" can make a visionary want to quit and just throw it all away.

However, this is why this prayer is here! It's time to break "it". Let's break the boundary!

Let's break the boundary of familiarity!
Let's break the boundary of frustration!
Let's break the boundary off of God!
Let's PRAY!

Prayer

Heavenly Father,

I come to you naked and unashamed. Father, today I bring my business(es) to you and surrender it/them into your hands. Father, I thank You for vision! I thank You for trusting me with vision, capability, imagination, and accessibility! I thank You for manifestation and completeness in who You have created me to be! Today I come to You God, repenting for every act of disobedience and distrust. Even now I come against the lack of boundary that has birthed disrespectful familiarity and bred frustration. God, I lift up every business owner now, who like me, has been afraid to push or try again! I lift them up to You! I lift myself up to You!

For every business owner who's felt abused or misused in this process, I lift them up!

For every business owner who woke up this morning and said, "I can't deal with this," and turned away from their dream, I lift them up!

Father, I pray even now that you will wipe the dust, frustration, and sadness off me and my business(es)! Even as You eliminate the familiarity and frustrations, I rely on Your Word which tells me that You will give me beauty for my ashes! God, I make the exchange today! I give You the ashes of my frustrations and processes, my bitterness and pain and ask for the EXCHANGE! Lord, I ask that the beauty of who You are will fill me even now. May a fresh fire of desire for the visions you have entrusted to me, now be made manifest in me! I decree and declare that familiarity that crosses my boundaries and frustration will not be a part of my business(es). I speak to the spirit of entitlement and command that it fall at my feet even now!

I pray even now, that as I begin to take these limits off myself, I will shift into places that I have never been before. May courage arise right now—the courage that causes me to be able to walk in rooms I have never been in and accomplish major and mighty partnerships in your name! I will not be afraid to speak to those I have never met! I will speak in boldness and knowledge! Your Word says that I have the capacity to possess every place I step into. I ask you for more courage to set and enforce boundaries where needed for me to carry out the assignments that you have entrusted me with, in my life and in my business.

Therefore, I command that every stench of paralysis be removed from my business(es), and I declare freedom to MOVE! Shift my mind for this MOVEMENT!

I free my feet NOW! I will not be stagnant but instead make KINGDOM moves for Your Glory! Someone in this world needs what I have, and I position myself to answer!

Father, I repent now for every boundary I have applied to You! I ask that you would raise me back up now Lord…raise me up in power and authority! It is my desire to make You proud, and though my soul may be tired, my soul refuses to sit back die! May I make moves in this moment that will cause me to make You smile, make You blush and make You proud!

I take the limit off my increase! I shift into VALUE! Let me not be afraid of my value! I embrace the value I bring to the table! I receive the UPGRADE required for this next level of positioning! So, Lord, I give it to You…. I give it ALL to You!

*I thank You for the ACTIVE VICTORY that causes me to overcome negative boundaries and create positive ones! For Your glory alone………
AMEN!*

Mom Guilt

Darlene Higgs Hollis

Her children arise and call her blessed…
Proverbs 31:28

As mothers, our goal is to be the best and our children see us as that Proverbs 31 woman. Even though we don't have a manual. We are expected to fill so many roles in the lives of our families and friends. But as mothers especially, we want to make sure we are there. However, building a business is time-consuming and challenging. Many times, requiring us to spend more hours working than we did on our nine-to-five jobs, or more time in our home office if we still work a nine-to-five. Children just want their mother's attention so many times do not understand that we are not ignoring them, but we are facing a balancing act of building business and taking care of their needs.

Twelve years ago, when I became a single mom after being married for thirteen years, working a nine-to-five while also building my business, was a very challenging time for me. I felt so guilty many days when I would come home, help with homework and other needs for my children, but not feeling fully present because I knew I needed desperately to get things done for my business. I thought this would change when I began working full time in my business. No, this was not the case. My children seem to require my attention even more. All they saw was that mommy was at home. They did not hesitate to just walk into my office at any time and just start talking (sometimes I would be on a call) or wanting me to stop and listen to them or help with something. I would simultaneously be frustrated because my focus was interrupted and feeling guilty because we both felt like they were not getting the attention needed. Something had to give.

I prayed about how I felt and concluded that I had to set boundaries.

My children and I would have a weekly meeting just to share our thoughts, vent and pray for each other. At that week's meeting, I told my children how I felt; the importance of me balancing being there for them, as well as building my business. I set several boundaries so that we could move forward, and I was no longer constantly guilty, and they did not feel like I was not listening to them.

- I have office hours, and if my door is closed, that means do not come in nor knock. If it's an emergency, then text or knock on the door. Door closed meant I needed to be laser focused.

- If my soaking music is on, that definitely means DO NOT DISTURB.

- We set-up times weekly or daily for me to help with school assignments, sign papers or talk about anything concerning them that could not wait for our meeting.

They now respect that I am building a business and will sometimes work longer hours but will still be there for them. They just have to speak up if they need me. Or they will remind me if I forget.

Mom, I encourage you to find ways to set boundaries and activities that will work for you and your family. If you have another adult in the household, see how they can support you.

Prayer

Lord, thank you for the gift of being a mother. I don't take that for granted. I also thank you for this marketplace ministry that you have given me. However, I am having a hard time balancing both. I am feeling the guilt of not being there for my children as much as I used to or as much as they want me to. Please give me strategies for being more present with my children as well as dong what is needed for this business you have given me to lead. Lord, please send more support in both areas so that I will not abort or give up. I ask you for strength to carry out both assignments well. Help me to be that mother whose children call her blessed. All these things I ask in Jesus' name. Amen.

Graced for Tiara

Anitra Truelove

But Ruth replied, "Don't urge me to leave you or to turn back from you. Where you go, I will go, and where you stay, I will stay. Your people will be my people and your God my God. Where you die, I will die, and there I will be buried. May the Lord deal with me, be it ever so severely, if even death separates you and me." When Naomi realized that Ruth was determined to go with her, she stopped urging her. So, the two women went on until they came to Bethlehem. When they arrived in Bethlehem, the whole town was stirred because of them, and the women exclaimed, "Can this be Naomi?"

Ruth 1:16-19 NIV

Over twelve years ago, a young lady, Tiara, joined our church after being invited by her friend. Her friend would go on and on about how much this young lady was like me and believed we needed to meet.

One evening while Tiara was just visiting our ministry, the Lord had me minister to her. A lot of past traumas were exposed as well as prophetic revelation about who she is in God's Kingdom. I later found out that her mother had been on drugs her entire life and lost her parental rights when Tiara was just three years old. Tiara was raised by her father and did not know how to be maternal and struggled with a spirit of rejection.

While Tiara was in college, her friend told me that Tiara was facing homelessness. I invited her to live with my family and me. During this time, the Lord gave me a dream of us in our old age and that she was my Ruth. God had me labor with her and speak words of deliverance over her life.

As time went on, I went through a divorce and faced the greatest challenges of my life. I was able to reap from her all that I had sown into her life. She helped me in several areas of my life when I was broken and while I was at my worst.

Today, she has inherited her niece because of her sister's death. Her niece, who is now being raised as her daughter and is the same age she was when her mother lost her rights. She is now fully equipped to raise her and has rewritten her DNA. Don't despise small beginnings because the one that you are pouring into can be the one who will be raised up to bless you and help you maneuver through life and business endeavors when you need it most. I now have a legacy that took me years to cultivate. Tiara is not my daughter by blood but my spiritual daughter in the Kingdom. My people are her people. What started out as a prophetic word that I was obedient to give turned into a journey that would grow us into spiritual formation and an example of generational transference.

I am now a life and business coach, motivational speaker, minister of the gospel and equipping others. Tiara and I have used our story to help many who have dealt with a spirit of rejection and abandonment. We also have a mission to help other women identity who their Naomi and/or Ruth is, teach them how to not self-sabotage, and help them birth what they are carrying. So, others will be blessed and stirred by their mandate.

Prayer

God, I thank you that you have chosen me to be a blessing to others; that you have chosen me to mentor other women in entrepreneurship. Help me to obey without delay when you tell me to share a word that would be a blessing for generations to come or coach other women to be successful in her business endeavors. Help me to operate in the fruits of the spirit and have long-suffering especially for those you have called me to. God help me to identify who my Ruth is so I can understand the purpose and not sabotage my connections. I dismantle pride that will keep me from receiving from those that you send to bless and help me to take my business to another level. I declare and decree that I will move in grace and find safety in what you have ordained. Remove walls and accusations that would try to come up against me and the God-given relationships that you put together. Thank you, Lord, that you will send those that are ordained to aid me in my family, business, and mandate in Jesus's name, Amen!

David had finished talking with Saul, Jonathan became one in spirit with David, and he loved him as himself. From that day Saul kept David with him and did not let him return home to his family. And Jonathan made a covenant with David because he loved him as himself. Jonathan took off the robe he was wearing and gave it to David, along with his tunic, and even his sword, his bow and his belt. 1 Samuel 18:1-4 NIV

In the Boat
With the G.O.A.T

Pretina Lowery

And a great windstorm arose, and the waves beat into the boat, so that it
was already filling. But He was in the stern, asleep on a pillow. And they
awoke Him and said to Him" Teacher, do you not care, that we are perish-
ing? "Then he arose and rebuked the wind, and said to the sea," Peace, be
still! And the wind ceased and there was a great calm.
Mark 4: 37-39 (NKJV)

How good are you at following instructions? Do you
follow immediately because of the person who has
given the command? Do you hesitate according to
how you feel at the time? Are you one who must know the outcome before you get yourself involved in the first place? Or do
you decline the offer entirely because you don't really trust going
somewhere other than where you've been or currently are? Could
you imagine the Savior inviting you to set sail with him on the
Love Boat? You were invited to sail with the G.O.A.T. (Greatest
of All Time)!

Nothing seems odd at the onset. The boat is holding the trav-
elers; the Master is resting and then low and behold, the waves
wave.

Can you think of a time that someone invited you somewhere, and all was going well until a fight broke out, they ran out of food, or you bumped into someone from your past? Did you automatically want to jump ship, or did you tough it out by drawing near to the one who escorted you to the affair?

Storms are inevitable. They are also invitations for Jesus to show his care. He stands up to calm you and the waves down.

It's interesting to me we will follow Siri but struggle to adhere to the beckoning of the One who is leading us to a destination of destiny. How many of us without an ounce of hesitation have traveled to cities, countries and churches we have never visited before, hoping to see the sights, delight in the delicacies and to hear a word of encouragement? Yet we grapple with God when conditions we deem not favorable present themselves. When Jesus gives us a command, He already knows how it will turn out, which is exactly why He gives the invitation in the beginning.

Jesus isn't looking for perfection. He's looking for participation and partnership. Will you get out of your comfort zone and get in the boat with the G.O.A.T.?

Prayer

Creator, forgive me for being so afraid that it silenced my hope in you. You have proven time and time again that there is nothing too hard for you. You are the Lord over all. The winds, the waves and everything else you created, including me, must obey you. Obedience operates hand in hand with faith; for without either, it is impossible to please you. You are the same Savior who was with the disciples in their despair. May I not be one who questions if you care about the cares in my life. For conflict is not the absence of concern. I know fully well that from the beginning, your every move on my behalf has been out of your dedication to me. If the wind and the waves do not stop being who they were created to be, nor should I. If Jesus can fall asleep during a storm, then so shall I. You were able to rest because you relied on your Father's power, may I do the same. Jesus you being in the boat with the disciples showed your devotion. You waking up to command the waves to lay down is a display of your devotion. Speaking to the inanimate objects in my life further dictates the depth of your care and devotion toward me. You alone calm the raging seas within me. May I be like the wind and receive great calm. When storms of doubt, uncertainty and confusion are surrounding me may I look to, draw near, and call upon the one who anchors my soul. Amen.

God's Vertical and Man's Horizontal

Dr. Roz Knighten-Warfield

Proverbs 3:5-12 (MSG)

The Bible is awesome when it comes to the teaching of our 1/1 time with the Father and our time with man. As I journey this faith walk, I'm learning that it is vital that I prioritize my vertical alignment with Daddy. I hope you don't mind my level of intimacy with Him. I would think to say that everybody is operating on a fast and furious schedule and it's easy to lose sight of what the true assignments are that Daddy has assigned.

His will or our will? That is the true question at hand! In my 6.2 chapters of my life, I'm still developing true north to stay in God's Lane and not mine. The vertical alignment with Daddy is so important. It requires hearing His voice. This may come by intentional acts of gratitude, prayer, hydration, Bible Study and knowing your God assignments.

I have another question. Let's track your day and see how you are spending your time and ask these questions. Do you trust the Holy Spirit to be the GPS system of your life? It's time to re-evaluate your days and stop kinking the water hose with activities that don't matter. Your vertical alignment is pointing in the direction, which reminds us Daddy knows best!

It's time to **SOAR!** *Surrender, Obey, Abide Radically* and yield to the Holy Spirit! Always think of the supernatural heroes as the Power Team of Three; Father, Son, and Holy Spirit are my **SON-shine** of hope. Yes, I spelled sunshine the way you see it! It has a lot of power.

Work your vertical alignment and pay attention to every opportunity that the Lord wakes you up, being full of gratitude that you are blessed. What are you asking? Are you already on your cell phone? Have you hit the snooze button several times? Well, this is a lot of good-for-nothing actions of no power and direction. It's time to ask for laser beam focus on a daily schedule of constant conversations of honor, integrity, and excellence with Daddy!

Try this and also make it look like you:

- Upon waking up, always give **praiZe** with a "z" for the zest of life that Daddy has allowed breathe into your nostrils one more time. That is what I call gratitude!

- Do you hear a song in your heart?

- **Hum, sing** and or **play some soaking music** that is instrumental to get you warmed up. Example: Commanding Your Day, Nathaniel Coe III https://youtu.be/SJIUWc1Smpo

  o Best if on a recorder or ipod, so you are not distracted and tempted to go visit social media.

  o Preparation and planning is KING!

- **Hydrate like a fresh baptismal.** If you have not been drinking your water, begin today and monitor your intake until you are half your body's weight. Trust the process!
- **Bible Study**—not just your devotional, nonetheless pure word. Chew, Chew, Chew!
- Lastly and you thought I'd forgot, trust Daddy to take His providential hand and turn the dial from vertical to horizontal and give you your assignments with man and the world.

Prayer

Daddy, forgive me that I've not prioritized my time honoring you and myself. I call out and command the dismissal of squandering precious time. I hear your voice to lead, direct and guide. I will keep a S.M.I.L.E. vertically and horizontally. I decree to Simply Make Intentional Love Encounters, starting with myself first under the wise counsel of the Father, Son, and Holy Spirit the Supernatural Heroes. In Jesus' name! Amen.

Leading With Wisdom

Latesha Higgs

Let the wise listen and add to their learning, and let the discerning get guidance.

Proverbs 1:5 (NIV)

Wisdom extends beyond making sound decisions or profound sayings. Wisdom is a mindset that is grounded in our relationship with our Lord and Savior, Jesus Christ, and begins with our reverence for His limitless power and love. When we develop a wisdom mindset, we recognize our own limitations and rely on the guidance of our omniscient Father. As we grow in wisdom, we are better at discerning how to effectively apply the principles of God's Word in every area of our life and business. Having a wisdom mindset does not stop you completely from making mistakes—nobody is perfect. However, with a wisdom mindset, you'll better discern and quickly learn from the lesson when the mistake is made. Remember, a mistake is only a failure when you didn't learn the lesson.

As entrepreneurs, Executive Directors, CEOs and leaders in our respective fields, a wisdom mindset is a must. Without it, we cannot effectively build relationships, leverage our influence and lead God's people the way He has instructed us. In fact, wisdom is what Solomon asked for and recognized he needed from God to lead his people. To do the good work which God prepared in advance for us to do requires that we seek His wisdom and guidance daily. While we don't know what the day may bring, what will happen at the meeting, or have all the answers, He does. As Lord of our lives, He is our ultimate leader and knows exactly what we need, and who we need to become, to execute His plans for our life. That's right, become. Wisdom also helps us to become the leader we need to be to carry out our divine assignment in the fields in which He has called us to serve. Serving as a leader of a business requires that we prepare our heart, mind, and spirit to lead with love, humility, and, most of all, wisdom.

Prayer

Dear Heavenly Father,

Your wisdom is unmatched, your glory is beyond words. I thank you for your instruction and guidance. Lord, I thank you for trusting me to lead this business and lead your people. Dear Lord, to lead your people effectively, like Solomon, I ask for wisdom. I seek wisdom in Jesus' name to not only lead your people effectively, but to be an impactful leader to myself. Lord, I know and recognize that the most difficult person to lead and guide is me. So, Lord, grant me the wisdom to lead myself and the humility to follow your lead with diligence. Lord, besides wisdom, send people into my life who will lovingly and truthfully mentor and guide me; open my eyes to recognize them. Prepare my heart to receive them and the instructions they give me. Lord, heal my heart of past hurts and trauma so that I will not take their lessons as offenses, but in wisdom use it to lead me on righteous paths. Lord open doors of opportunity for me to meet people who can mentor and guide me to be an effective, impactful, and influential business leader and entrepreneur. Lord open my eyes to see who you have put in my life to direct and guide me. Open my ears to hear the truth. Lord strengthen my discernment so that I will know who is for me and who is not. Grant me favor with all those who will help me to become the woman and the business leader you have called me to be. Lord, keep me humble so that I will always stay in the posture of a student—learning and gleaning from those who have gone before me. Lord prepare my heart to receive your instructions and wisdom from wherever and whomever you send it. Remind me, Abba, to thirst for your wisdom and guidance and then Father, empower me to put into action all that I learn. Strengthen me to act on the instructions and wisdom you give so that I will not just be a hearer of your word but also a doer. Lord, I pray for wisdom to make better decisions in my organization, team, and life. Lord, I thank you for your grace and mercy during those days and times that I have fallen short and not walk in the paths you have instructed for me. Lord, in this learning season of my life, help me to stay patient and keep the right perspective while you do a great work in me. Help me to see the lessons I need to learn and apply. Keep my heart and mind focused on you and not what is going on around me—for you are bigger than my problems and all things will work together for good for me because I am called according to your purpose. Lord, as I grow in wisdom of your word, keep me focused on my calling and assignment and not on the mediocre and trivial things. Satan, I bind you in Jesus' name for I will NOT be distracted by anything that will pull me from doing God's work.

Heavenly Father, grant me the wisdom needed to discern the major things I need to concern myself with from those things that are minor. I declare on this day that I will not major in the minor. I plead the blood of Jesus over my mind, heart, and thoughts. Lord, grant me the wisdom needed to protect my ear gates (what I allow myself to hear), eye gates (what I allow myself to see), and mouth (what I tell myself). It's in your name Jesus that I pray and ask these things. Amen!

Leading But Experiencing Domestic Violence

Dorothea Robinson

Have I not commanded you? Be strong and courageous. Do not be afraid; do not be discouraged, for the Lord your God will be with you whenever you go.
Joshua 1:9 (KJV)

While many women have successful thriving businesses, there are many of them who also live a life of hurt and pain at home; known as domestic violence. You may be that woman.

Day in and day out, you have to show one face to the outside world, but you are living another reality at home. As a leader you are well-respected, but you experience the total opposite at home. You are praying and hoping that your two worlds don't collide. You don't ever want anyone to know the shame you carry.

This prayer is to encourage, uplift and cover those women business owners who can't seem to escape abuse at home. Domestic violence has even affected the small business owner to the multi-million-dollar business owner. Let this prayer offer hope and encouragement to get out and get free.

Prayer

Father, Most High God and lover of my soul, I come boldly before you always giving you praise and glory. I am thankful for the charge of the business that has been gifted to me. I am grateful for the opportunity to assist those clients that come to me for guidance, leadership, and coaching. Being in the position of a servant leader is an honor. Father, I thank you. As I count on your guidance in my business, I must also trust you in my home and personal life. I am going through so much hurt and pain, but I will remember what you have said about me. I will recall the scripture like Joshua 1:9 "Have I not commanded you? Be strong and courageous. Do not be afraid; do not be discouraged, for the Lord your God will be with you whenever you go." The painful and hurtful things that I am experiencing at home, your words and promises, bring me peace. Psalm 34:4 says, "You have delivered me from my fears."

As I have developed plans for the business, which have proven to be successful, I will also develop a plan to be free from the abusive conditions at home. I will safely but diligently create a plan to live a life of freedom. You say things about me that I will encourage myself with. I will gain strength minute by minute to break the cycle of abuse in my life, gaining amazing strength to be free from abuse.

Until that day that I finally free myself, I will praise you now for my prayers answered. I know you are in control and will answer my steadfast prayer for freedom, freedom from domestic violence. Amen.

For The People You Have Sent Me

Dorothea Robinson

For in fact the body is not one member but many.
1 Corinthians 12:14 (NKJV)

At some point in building your business, you realize that you cannot do it all on your own if you want your business to grow. Even when you know how to efficiently perform all tasks and functions that your business needs to operate, you will find that you are doing more harm than good because delays start occurring. You see a bottleneck. You eventually realize the need for a team in certain areas. Now you realize that you should be operating at the Chief Operating Officer and not as an employee of your business. Sometimes releasing parts of your business to others and trusting another person with your business baby is difficult.

This is where trust in the Lord to send the right people to help you in your business is key. The right team is beneficial for you as well as that employee or that contract worker. Continue to trust God through the process.

Prayer

Father,

From the very day you downloaded the idea of being a business owner, you have been with me. In time of amazing mind-blowing experiences—those days of not much happening to those days of "how am I going to get through this mess" days—you are there. I know you are with me always. You said in your Word, "Behold, I am with you, and will guard you in all places whither you go and will bring you again into this land; for I will not leave you until I have done that which I have spoken to you of. (Genesis 28:15-15) "I will never leave you nor forsake you!" Taking comfort in these words, I remind myself that I can always count on you!

As my business grows, I want to thank you for the people you have sent me to work beside me in my business. Because you have brought them to me to help grow my business to its fullest potential, because I trust in you, I am fully aware that I am responsible to them, not for them.

So, Father, with each skill that they possess, I respect and honor their gifts. I ask you today to touch and guide each one of them in their lives and as they work to bring my vision to fruition.

Help us to work seamlessly together as a well-oiled machine. Help me to lead but still be open to what you show my team for my business. Let respect and an atmosphere of free creativity permeate my team. I bind up dissention among my team. Create an atmosphere of free, but respectful speech. I pray that each member of my team will experience professional as well as personal growth as a result of being a part of the _____(name of my business) experience.

Father, I thank you in advance for the positive outcome for the mission of my business, for the employees that came together to see business reach its

116

goal as well as for the new downloads you have given the company to move through the next exciting journey. God, I thank you in advance for the answers to this prayer. Amen.

MONEY

No More Money Drama!

Monique Caradine-Kitchens

How tithing and building a strong money foundation will help you end your
struggle with money and unlock your overflow.

Bring the whole tithe into the storehouse, that there may be food in my house.
Test me in this," says the LORD Almighty, "and see if I will not throw
open the floodgates of heaven and pour out so much blessing that there will
not be room enough to store it.
Malachi 3:10 (NIV)

Even though I was born and raised in Chicago, I had
never been to the top of the world-famous Willis Tower
(formerly Sears Tower). I grew up seeing the buildings
on the city skyline all my life and my mom even worked there for
a while, but I had never been to the top. That all changed on January 1, 2016.

You see, a few years earlier we packed up and moved to
Puerto Rico, so this particular year, my son and I decided to return
to our hometown for a holiday visit. I wanted us to start the New
Year by getting a view of Chicago from one of its highest

elevations. Together, I wanted us to look out from that breathtaking vantage point and know that anything was possible for us!

The trip to the 108th floor was cool enough by itself, but I did not know that on the way to the top we would get a history lesson about how the building was built. A brief documentary that played in a small theater on one of the lower levels explained that before construction workers could start building what was once the tallest skyscraper in the world, they had to first build downward.

Even though most people can't see it, the foundation is the most important part of that building. It took more than a year to build the massive structure, which goes 100 feet below the surface of the ground and required the use of dozens of other components made of steel and cement. The designers of this historic building knew that if the tower was going to withstand the test of time (and weather) in the windy city, a strong and unshakeable foundation had to be put in place before workers could build upward.

As I watched the documentary, something clicked. It dawned on me that for many women, the lack of a strong foundation is just one element that can lead to money drama.

That's when I knew that a part of my work would need to focus on helping women create a solid money foundation. I believe that every woman should be able to leave a financial legacy for her family and set them up to never have to worry about money again.

So, I immediately went to work to create specific coaching programs that are still in place in my practice today. The goal of the programs is to help you build a wealth foundation by giving you the tools to do five things:

1. Create wealth by giving you ideas for new income streams.
2. Transfer your wealth by establishing a will and trust to hold your valued assets.
3. Eliminate debt including credit cards, student loans, mortgages, cars, or any other form of debt that is burdensome.
4. Save money. I was surprised to find out that many of the women I've worked with didn't have a basic savings account in place. If that's the case for you, it's okay! There is no judgment here. As a coach, my job is to help you create the habit of saving regularly so that by the end of three months or six months, a year or whatever you decide, you will be able to celebrate the progress that you make!
5. Tithe. Tithing is a biblical mandate. Even though we live under grace, thanks to our Lord and Saviour, Jesus himself mentions tithing in the New Testament and encourages us to continue this powerful practice. Matt 23:23. Tithing is still important today and I believe it (combined with fasting, prayer and communion with God) has the power to break every stronghold we have EVER faced. Tithing is something I believe we must recommit to, and we must make it a non-negotiable part of our money foundation.

The reality of foundation building.

Without a strong foundation, nothing we build will last through difficult times – not our relationships, not our business, family, or our financial future. Just imagine not knowing if your house could withstand a thunderstorm or a blizzard. Imagine always having to wonder what would happen if the weather called for sustained high winds? The fear of your house literally blowing away would have you living in a constant state of worry. Well, the same applies to your money.

With a strong wealth foundation, you never have to worry if a large, unexpected expense comes up or if you want to splurge on a nice vacation or if you get ill and can't make decisions on your own. You just never know what kind of curve ball life is going to throw your way, so a solid foundation helps you to be prepared no matter what.

The problem with foundations though is they require the dirty, most un-sexy kind of work there is.

When it comes to making sure your money foundation is built to last, you will have to confront your old money story. You'll have to face past money mistakes. You'll have to restore your credit, cut back on impulse buying and start saving money. You'll also have to start tracking your income and expenses rather than playing a guessing game about what's coming in and going out. Truth be told, you might even need to get some help with all of this.

Most people don't jump out of bed in the morning, excited to do this kind of work. I know I don't! However, what I do like is the feeling I have knowing that when I roll up my sleeves and get really in-tune with my money, I will reap the benefits. I also know that when tithing is a part of my money foundation, the Lord will do what he promised in Malachi 3:10-12 when he said:

> *Bring the whole tithe into the storehouse, that there may be food in my house. Test me in this," says the LORD Almighty, "and see if I will not throw open the floodgates of heaven and pour out so much blessing that there will not be room enough to store it. I will prevent pests from devouring your crops, and the vines in your fields will not drop their fruit before it is ripe," says the LORD Almighty. "Then all the nations will call you blessed, for yours will be a delightful land," says the LORD Almighty.*

Imagine being able to build a large amount of wealth in a very short amount of time. Imagine being able to assist family members if needed and being able to send your children to college debt free. Imagine being able to give generously to causes you believe in! Then imagine how it feels knowing that when troubles come, your wealth can stand strong and your faith in God will be even stronger. Let that be the feeling that fuels you as you make the commitment to building your money foundation.

Prayer

Heavenly Father, you are the Alpha, the Omega, the beginning, and the end. I lift up Your name above every name and I give you praise! Thank you for being the source of my supply!

Father, you said in your word in Luke 10:19 that you have given me all power and authority to trample on snakes and scorpions and over all the power of the enemy; and that nothing at all will harm me. You said in Ephesians 1:19 that the same power that raised Jesus from the dead lives on the inside of me. So right now, Father I exercise my authority, I reclaim my dominion and I declare that I AM more than a conqueror. I declare that I am the head and NOT the tail. I declare that because I am building a strong money foundation and I am recommitting to tithing that you are throwing open the floodgates of heaven and pouring out so much blessing that I will not have room enough to store it.

I declare that I am the personification of God's awesome and creative power. I am a brilliant and beautiful work of art. There is perfection, power, excellence, wisdom, and courage bursting forth through me even as we speak, and today I declare and decree that I am overcoming lack in all its forms.

I speak to every money mountain in my life, and I command it to MOVE! I am becoming debt free. Big opportunities are coming to me now. I am breaking free of my money fears, and I am recognizing my worth. I open my mind and welcome profitable ideas, witty inventions, and new opportunities. I declare that these divine opportunities will give me the ability to enjoy more freedom and help transform the lives of others starting today.

I thank you God that because you have given me the authority to activate your word in my life, I hereby declare a new level of grace and ease in my business. I declare that I have favor in my workplace. I declare and decree that I am coming into a season where worldly rules do not apply to me. I live in the Kingdom economy! I flourish in the Kingdom economy! Doors are opening, supernatural access is being granted. I am drenched in God's favor, and my overflow is right here, right now, and I boldly claim it, in Jesus' name!

Don't Quit

E. Laquanda Whitehead-Grady

And I am certain that God, who began the good work within you, will continue his work until it is finally finished on the day when Christ Jesus returns.
Philippians 1:6 (NLT)

September 9, 1999, was the start of the entrepreneurial journey that would serve thousands with a God-given passion I never knew I possessed. I am the owner of LQ's Desktop Publishing, LLC, where I provide custom design publishing, printing, and business services for individuals and businesses nationwide. At the inception of my business, I began working with funeral homes by providing auxiliary printing services for families during their time of bereavement. This was a service I was already providing from time to time for friends and family who requested it. This was nothing new to me, only now I was providing such services on a larger scale to the funeral homes who needed full-service design, printing and even delivery of memorial brochures/programs to aid in fulfilling final arrangements for the families they served.

Business began with an explosion! I did not realize that funeral homes needed a specialty printing service dedicated to a quick turnaround time at a moment's notice. I knew God had placed me in a unique position in business. It was just a matter of how do I keep up? God blessed the works of my hands and LQ's Desktop Publishing gained the reputation for funeral printing in the local area, surrounding counties and beyond.

But as the years progressed, I realized that over the warmer months of the year, funeral printing waned, and revenue declined, and at times there was nothing at all. After several years of this pattern, I noted the primary source of income; when it was abundant and when it declined. I discovered a large portion of business revenue was from funeral printing and that funeral services are more active during the colder months of the year (i.e., Death rates increase during colder months of the year 1).

It was during these times that I wondered whether I should continue this business, providing these services, when I could not depend on it for year-round financial stability. At times, I would get so far behind in business expenses that even when business flourished again in the fall and winter months, it seemed that I was only working to pay past due expenses and never really making a profit. I seriously considered just closing the business to get a full-time 9-5 job where a weekly, bi-weekly, or even monthly check would be a dependable source of income. However, it was during these times God would remind me of Philippians 1:6 (NLT) "... that God, who began the good work within you, will continue his work until it is finally finished on the day when Christ Jesus returns."

I knew I could not quit.

I could not give up.

God began this work in me.

My gifts, talents, and abilities are His will working within me. I didn't start it. HE did! And HE will complete it! I can't give up. I can't close my business. I can't walk away. I can't give up!

Prayer

Dear Lord,

Starting this business wasn't easy. And at times, I wonder if I should just give up and let it all go. I am tired of wondering if or when my finances will stabilize and multiply. But Lord, as I pray this prayer, I am reminded of the desire YOU put in my heart to begin this work, to start this business. I am reminded of how YOU turned every enemy into my footstool and no weapon formed, prospered. I am reminded of every need you somehow provided. Every debt you paid. So, Lord, I trust you to complete the work YOU began in me. As YOU encouraged Joshua, so will I be strong. I will be very courageous. I will follow your Word, knowing that as I follow your Word, I will be successful in everything I do. I will not give up. You began this work and I trust you to complete it in Jesus' name. Amen.

Scripture References: Philippians 1:6 NLT; Joshua 1:7 NLT
Psalm 110:1 KJV

1 In recent years, U.S. death rates in winter months have been 8 to 12 percent higher than in non-winter months. Much of this increase relates to seasonal changes in behavior and the human body, as well as increased exposure to respiratory diseases. Jul 18, 2021. https://www.epa.gov/climate-indicators/climate-change-indicators-cold-related-deaths#

Processes and Systems

Altovise Pelzer

The tongue can bring death or life; those who love to talk will reap the consequences.

Proverbs 18:21 NLT

L ike any well-oiled machine, when things are out of alignment, it can create delays and distractions. The same can happen in our business. Praying over your processes and systems keeps your ear to God's mouth concerning your business.

Prayer 1

I speak to anything that has been clogging the systems within my business. I speak to whatever has been causing my systems to rust or corrode. Lord, I ask you to bring forth new systems or restore the systems that I currently have. Bestow upon me understanding and wisdom so I know how things work in alignment with your plan for my business. Remove the physical, emotional, and spiritual challenges that have clogged the system. These challenges have no dominion or power in my business or life. It will not be something I desire. It will not be something I go after.

Romans 8:28, says, *"And we know that God causes everything to work together for the good of those who love God and are called according to his purpose for them."* So, I walk in my purpose! I pray for my purpose! I speak my purpose! Every system that I use must fall into alignment with the purpose that you have for my business. Nothing will be out of place. Father, I lay my business at your feet so that you may tap back into place anything that has slipped or popped out. Restore the intersections of my business that are worn down from misuse.

Father, show me where I need to have replacements. Show me the systems and processes that need fresh energy like new batteries. My systems will not move slowly in this season. The client acquisition process, the customer journey, workflow, email automation, marketing, and follow up work are in alignment so that my brand stays in position to serve.

I ask all these things in Jesus' name. Amen!

Prayer 2

Like the intricate parts of a clock, Father, I speak that the people in my business work in alignment. Any pieces that need to be replaced are coming from my heavenly account, and I will not fear the changes that are necessary to keep my business running smoothly. Thank you for the replacements and upgrades.

Father, I thank you for a fresh fire in my life that ignites something fresh in my business and relationships. Idleness, gossip, unforgiveness, jealousy, and comparison will not distract or disengage the process of communication within my business. Creativity flows like rushing rivers within my business *partnerships. Faith filled mentors stand as dams and riverbanks to protect what you have blessed me to steward over.*

1 Peter 2:9 (NLT) says, "But you are not like that, for you are a chosen people. You are royal priests, a holy nation, God's very own possession. As a result, you can show others the goodness of God, for he called you out of the darkness into his wonderful light."

Therefore, I will not chase popularity, nor will I forsake values for volume. Instead, I chase after you daily through prayer and meditation. Kingdom connections are not orchestrated by luck or by popularity but by the blood shed for me on Cavalry. My business functions well and will not be seen as a replica of another business. My systems are God breathed and are uniquely created for me. You placed it on the inside of me even before I was placed into my mama.

Father, forgive me for tampering with anything according to my understanding of it. I will not walk in "good enough" this season when I serve a God that offers me more than enough. Basic and average are no longer the address where I live. I thank you for putting me in a position to handle more.

I ask all these things in Jesus' name. Amen.

Vision: Own Your Brand

Kenria Kelly

In the beginning God created the heavens and the earth. Now the earth was formless and empty, darkness was over the surface of the deep, and the Spirit of God was hovering over the waters. And God said, "Let there be light," and there was light.
Genesis 1:1-3

As a prayer strategist, I believe it is imperative to know the unseen warfare surrounding your life and brand. Moreover, I realize that many people have a vision and a dream, but before God's purpose for their life can come to fruition, their life has to be saturated with a level of confidence that comes through prayer. A vision gives insight into what is coming, a vision births expectancy.

Vision gives you foreknowledge of your future. However, nobody can effectively own their brand without having a vision. God alone births godly vision. It doesn't matter what you are experiencing, if you hold on, God will bring the vision to pass. We get our first glimpse of this in Genesis 1:1-3. Vision allowed God to see beyond what existed. The earth was formless, empty, and dark, but the Spirit of God moved and activated the atmosphere so that when God said, "Let there be light," there was light!

God had a vision, and His vision determined what His plans would be. God wanted a relationship with man; therefore, He created Adam. Genesis chapter 1 reveals that God the Creator put everything in place before He created man on the sixth day.

Once you have a godly vision, God will ensure that things will come together favorably if you are faithful. I would like to draw your attention once again to Genesis 1: 1-3

Now the earth was formless and empty, darkness was over the surface of the deep, and the Spirit of God was hovering over the waters. And God said, "Let there be light," and there was light.

When the spirit of God is hovering, that indicates faith and action. You must exercise faith.

You must exemplify the characteristics of Jesus Christ.

You must press on and find strategies to make certain that the vision God has given you will come to pass.

Adam was a brand that was unlike any other.

You are a brand that is unique, and unlike any other.

But what are you doing about the gifts and talents that God has placed in your hands?

Do you have a vision for your business?

Do you have a vision for your life?

If your answer is yes, do you believe God gave you this vision? Some dreams and visions are not of God, but if you know God has given you a business idea or assignment, it will come to fruition if you are faithful. Undoubtedly, it is wise to become cognizant of this: in whatever area God has assigned you to, you must become knowledgeable about.

At this time, I would like to draw your attention to a beautiful young lady by the name of Esther. Esther had to be groomed for twelve months before going into the presence of the king. Esther 2:12, says,

Before a young woman's turn came to go in to King Xerxes, she had to complete twelve months of beauty treatments prescribed for the women, six months with oil of myrrh and six with perfumes and cosmetics.

Esther was predestined to be queen to save the Jews, but she had to go through a process. Yea though you walk through dark seasons, God will never leave or forsake you. Hold on! All of your sacrifices are not in vain.... God will bring you through. When one door closes, another door opens. You must go the extra mile. You will press your way through.

Be encouraged by the Lord, and in the power of his might. Genesis 2:15 states:

The Lord God took the man and put him in the Garden of Eden to work it and take care of it.

Saints of God it is your responsibility to take care of what God has given you. Do business the right and just way. Do business God's way. In the marketplace, some of your competitors may utilize unjust strategies and measures, but when you are owning your brand, integrity should always be the key part of the process. Your brand is what people think about when they think about your business or company. As a 'Kingdom Entrepreneur', integrity, quality and dedication are some adjectives that should come to mind when people consider your business as an option. When you own your brand, you want to ensure that your business upholds high standards and good Christian ethics.

Finally, prayer brings clarity to vision, and along with market research, quality products and ethical choices help to create a sustainable brand. Prayer should never be taken lightheartedly for it is the portal that allows us to remain connected to God. Prayer helps to set the atmosphere that we desire to permeate our businesses and in our hearts. As you declare this prayer time, God is going to download strategic insight and revelation. God will help you to know, how and when to move. God wants you to no longer see yourself as an ordinary being, but as an extraordinary human being, who is doing Kingdom business. There will be a paradigm shift in your life and business, but you must have the faith to believe.

Prayer

Dear Heavenly and most esteemed Father I come before you this day, in steadfast agreement with Jeremiah 29:11, "For I know the plans I have for you," declares the LORD, "plans to prosper you and not to harm you, plans to give you hope and a future." I believe that your will is not only for me to effectively execute my brand, but to perfect the gifts and talents that you have implanted deep within me. Teach me, oh Lord, the true purpose of my brand and connect me with earthly angels who will help to deposit divine guidelines and strategies that will help to propel me forward.

Dear Lord, your will is for me to prosper and do well in the areas that you have assigned to me. Help me know my brand and master my brand, so that I can prosper and be a perpetual conduit of blessings to the Kingdom of God. Who I am, and who I will become, was predestined even before I was conceived in my mother's womb, therefore I realize that my life and destiny is not just about me knowing my brand, but to own my brand. Father God, I come against doubt and unbelief.

I will not falter.

I will not fail.

I break the spirit of procrastination and limitation.

I will not minimize my brand.

I will not minimize my grace.

I am well able.

I will not fear.

I will not break under pressure.

I will not breakdown, but I will break through.

Today I made a conscious decision to thrive in every area of life and in my business.

I declare that answers and solutions are coming to me now.

I declare investors are being released to me now.

Destiny helpers and divine connections.

I will cultivate the right relationships.

I will manage my affairs well.

I will be a good steward over all that you have entrusted me with.

Every need related to my life and business is being supplied now, in Jesus' name.

Today I put on new wings; I soar like an eagle.

I see things differently.

I approach things differently.

Divine wisdom is my portion.

I receive peace now because I know all things are working together for my good.

God has elevated me above my trials.

God has elevated me above my battles.

I walk in the newness of God.

According to 3 John 1:2, I prosper, and I am in good health.

I release my name in the heavenlies today.

I employ the blood of Jesus Christ.

Every barrier has been broken.

Every chain falls now.

Every battle cease in the name of Jesus Christ of Nazareth.

Today I turn a new chapter.

Today I receive freedom.

Today I walk in liberty.

Today I own my brand and become one with the vision and mandate that God has for my life in Jesus' name.

It's A Matter of Time

TuRhonda Freeman

My times are in Your hand.
Psalm 31:15a (NKJV)

Timing is everything. More often than not, we spend more time waiting for the right moment than we do enjoying the "now" moment. We write out the vision. We set realistic goals. We put in the time and effort to see the vision to fruition. And then we wait.

Will you agree that waiting is the most challenging part of the process? Of course, it is.

I specifically remember when waiting was the last thing I wanted to do. Here's my story:

I built the business. I did everything right. I didn't cut any corners. I prayed, fasted, meditated, and dedicated it all to God. Then I waited for the success. But nothing happened. Actually, it seemed to get worse every single day. I relied heavily on the notion that 'if you build it, they will come'. I sat perched at the window, waiting for my present reality to make it all make sense. While I was growing the most precious miracle inside my physical body, turmoil and disappointments were happening on the outside.

Tears became my norm. I weighed my options and walking away felt like the most natural solution. How could I birth a miracle in all of this mess? The anxiety of "what now" swarmed my heart and became the only thing that I could feast on.

Then, one day, everything changed. The negotiations began, and it all seemed unreal.

Then I waited some more. Paperwork, legalities, red tape and more waiting.

Finally, on the day that I was due to give birth to my miracle baby, I signed a business deal that made my head swim. All my waiting had led me to one day that changed my life forever. And God's grace had the final say!

Do you believe that God has already set your times and seasons?

Do you believe that the success of your business happens in due time?

When God makes you wait, here are some promises:
- You are heard. - Psalm 40:1
- You are blessed. - Isaiah 30:18
- You experience His goodness. - Lamentations 3:25
- You will not be ashamed. - Psalm 25:3, Isaiah 49:23
- Your strength will be renewed. - Isaiah 40:31
- You will inherit the earth. - Psalm 37:9
- You will be saved. - Proverbs 20:22, Isaiah 25:9
- You will receive the glorious things God has prepared for you. – Isaiah 64:4

REPEAT AFTER ME:

Today, I declare that my times and seasons are in God's hands. I am not afraid of what is coming because He is in complete control.

Today, I surrender my time to the Lord.

I surrender everything that has a time limit and an expiration date in my life and business. I declare that I will arrive at the right place at the right time. There are no failures, delays, or disappointments that can keep me out of God's perfect timing. My best days are not behind me, but they are unfolding right before my eyes. I declare that the events of my life have been preparing me for this moment in time. I declare that it is only a matter of time before my gifts make room for me. It is only a matter of time before all things work together for my good. It is only a matter of time before the words that I speak manifest into the life that I envision. It is only a matter of time before grace has the final say.

Today, I cast out fear, anxiety, impatience, frustration, and doubt. I declare that God's timing is the perfect time. And it is so.

Amen!

Time Management

Coleen Ifill Nipper

See then that you walk circumspectly, not as fools but as wise, redeeming the
time, because the days are evil. Therefore do not be unwise, but understand
what the will of the Lord is.

Ephesians 5:15-17 (NKJV)

S etting goals and prioritizing tasks are vital when it pertains
to time management. Make it a practice to structure your
day to ensure that you are intentionally working on something that is directly associated with your assignment. Put specific
strategies in place that will help you stay on tasks and create realistic goals for you to accomplish. Remember that time is money!

Prayer

God, as I come to you this day, Father, presenting all my plans to you, I
would first like to say thank you for giving me another opportunity to be in
the land of living. Thank you, Father, because there is none like you. I thank
you God for choosing me and for calling me Father to fulfill this assignment
(Name of business or ministry) here on earth. So, God, today as I come to
you, presenting all things pertaining to my management of time, let me first
ask that you bless me with wisdom. Show me just what you need me to do,

God. I ask you to help me be a good steward of my time. Lord, my desire is that I would not use my time unwisely, but that I would have the wisdom to know how to allocate my time effectively and efficiently. I place every area of my life in your hands so that I am obedient in the things that you have called me to do. Lord, your Word says that a good man's steps are ordered by you, so I'm asking father to please order my steps. I pray in the mighty name of Jesus that you would grant me favor in my business and ministry endeavors. Bless every task that needs to be fulfilled and bless whatever doors you allow to open or to birth from relationships formed from my business or ministry. Help me to never forget that my assignment is a God-ordained assignment. So, allow me to use my time wisely. Help me use my tools successfully and let me never move ahead of your timing. Let me never operate on my own, but allow the Holy Spirit to lead, guide and direct me into all truth.

Father, I give you my mind today so that I have your mindset. You are my planner, so I will give you my plans. I give you my will so that your will is done through me as I manage my time and my tasks wisely. I come against the spirit of procrastination and distraction. I come against anything that may hinder me from being progressive in you. God, I send all those things right now back to the very pits of hell and I declare, and decree from this day forward, Lord, that I will use my time wisely. I declare and decree that whatever I do, Lord that you will divinely orchestrate it. I will wait for your instructions so that I know what to do, when to do it and how it should be done. God, I present my business and ministry to you. I ask that you take charge of them right now in the name of Jesus. Lord God, I give to you all that I am struggling with in my business and ministry, especially in my time management. Oh God I present those issues to you Father because I believe that you can do all things but fail. Help me to stay the course, remove the spirit of feeling that I have missed my time, or that I have wasted time. Redeem back time to me and remind me that you operate in the fullness of time. Grant me the strength and wisdom that I need to be successful, in the mighty name of Jesus. Amen.

Reminder to Self

As a business owner and as a ministry leader, I must be able to set limits and boundaries with everything that I am tasked to do. I cannot forget to ask God to continue to order my steps. I must make sure that whatever I am doing that I am in God's will. I need to also ensure that I am in full alignment with His will concerning my business and my ministry. I must develop a sense of discipline especially in the areas of my life that I know I need to be disciplined in. I must not waste my time on things that are not within the scope of my purpose.

It's Working for Your Good

E. Laquanda Whitehead-Grady

And we know that all things work together for good to those who love God,
to those who are the called according to His
purpose.
Romans 8:28 (KJV)

I haven't always been an entrepreneur, even though I knew I wanted to one day start my business. I just didn't have a clue what that business would be. When I graduated from college, I thought I wanted to teach, so I took the Teaching Certification Test (TCT) and passed it with no education classes or educational degree to my credit. But I figured, if I taught, I could do so provisionally while completing the teaching certification requirements to obtain a Clear renewal Certificate. In the meantime, I began substitute teaching, and because I held a bachelor's degree, they placed me in a long-term teaching position. I quickly discovered after two years in the classroom that teaching kids would not be the best fit for my career choice.

I continued my search for employment and found it with a hotel corporation as an auditor. Still desiring to one day establish my own business, in 1998, I placed an ad in the "Big Yellow

Book" i.e., the yellow pages. Because of the magnitude of the circulation of this publication during that time, and the many business listings that would be published in it, I had to pay to place the ad a year in advance and a monthly fee for a year after it was in print. At this time, I only had a desire for entrepreneurship and the faith to place the ad. I placed the ad, and then I forgot about it and continued to work as an auditor.

I had been there for about a year and a half when the hotel was sold, and they hired a new general manager. He brought in his own people. One of which he asked me to train. One night when I arrived, I was told that I was no longer needed and on September 7, 1999, they terminated me. The one I had been training would take my position. I had no idea I had been training my replacement! Shocked and in disbelief, I could not understand what had just happened. I knew I would move on to further my career someday, but I always thought it would be on my terms. However, God had other plans.

That night, as I went to sleep, I felt the arms of the Lord as he wrapped me in His love and compassion. It was His comfort that let me know it would all work for my good. I slept peacefully that night.

Two days later, I received a phone call asking if this was LQ's Desktop Publishing? With some hesitation, while having to think about what she said, she continued by saying that she was looking at the ad in Yellow Pages and wanted to know if I could print the program booklets for her Pastor's Anniversary. It was then I remembered the ad I placed a year ago. I told her "Yes" I could do it!

But guess what? I had no computer, no printer, no desk, no supplies. What had I just done? I said "yes", in faith and it was faith that mobilized me to fulfill the first order for the establishment of LQ's Desktop Publishing. The ad I placed in faith a year earlier and had forgotten about, was now the catalyst that catapulted me into entrepreneurship. Although I lost my job, I found my passion.

Today, over twenty-two years later LQ's Desktop, LLC is still in business and standing strong. *"And we know that all things work together for good to those who love God, to those who are the called according to His purpose"* (Romans 8:28).

Prayer

Dear Lord,

Although I don't always understand why circumstances happen the way they do, help me remember that "all things work together for good... to those who are called according to His purpose." Lord when I don't know how or I don't understand why, help me find comfort in knowing that it is all about your purpose for my life and my business. You have a plan and a purpose for me. Your plan will prosper me. Therefore, it is your will that I want to prevail in my life. This is a business you birthed through me. Every challenge serves to stretch me. Every triumph serves to encourage me. Every mistake serves to enrich me. Every client/customer is a ministry. Every day I am walking in the call to Your purpose. Every task propels me to my divine destiny. Thank you for the plans you have for me, that are good, and that your expected end is the purpose you have for my life. Thank you for your purpose being fulfilled in me and through me in the lives of others. My journey as an entrepreneur is Your purpose fulfilled. And I thank you that all things are working together for my good because I am called according to Your purpose, in Jesus' name. *AMEN.*

Scripture References Jeremiah 29:11 NIV, Romans 8:28 KJV

Strategy

Shaundra Straughter

For the vision is yet for an appointed time, but at the end it shall speak, and not lie: though it tarry, wait for it, because it will surely come, it will not tarry."
Habakkuk 2:3 KJV

Blessed is the man that walketh not in the counsel of the ungodly, nor standeth in the way of sinners, nor sitteth in the seat of the scornful. But his delight is in the law of the LORD; and in his law doth he meditate day and night. And he shall be like a tree planted by the rivers of water, that bringeth forth his fruit in his season; his leaf also shall not wither; and whatsoever he doeth shall prosper.
Psalm 1:1-3

Running a business can be daunting, especially if there is no clear vision or guidance for how the business will be ran for it to be successful. The road of entrepreneurship is not for the weak and requires keen attention to details and a firm establishment in strategy. "Where there is no vision, the people perish (Proverb 29:18 KJV)." This scripture transcends various areas of our lives. Habakkuk 2:3 (KJV) encourages us to write the vision and make it plain. For our desires concerning our business and our lives to become guiding principles that establish well-built foundations, we must WRITE THE VISION. In doing so, we must not become fearful of what we see for our lives and businesses in the months and years to come! There is nothing too hard for God. What is your vision in this season of your life? Have you written it as you've seen it? Vision requires sight and some imagination. Don't be afraid to imagine yourself as successful. See yourself as an influence in the marketplace, a leading company, and an innovative resource to consumers locally and abroad. WRITE THE VISION.

Not only do we need to write the vision, but we must also be open to strategy. Vision alone is not enough as faith alone is not enough. What will you need to make the vision come to pass? STRATEGY.

James 2:14-26 (KJV) declares that *"Faith without works is dead."* It's not enough for us to settle for a written vision. We must work towards what we see. Strategy provides us with an action plan that ensures we have the necessary steps to get to our destination. It's a game plan, a blueprint, our operating policies and procedures; the tactics we will utilize to produce results. Strategy provides us with the knowledge needed for what to do and what not to do in the world of business operation. Psalm 1:1-3 (KJV) decrees that we will be blessed when we do not walk in agreement with ungodly counsel or take fellowship with those that know so much until you can't tell them anything. It goes on to tell us that when we focus on the Word of God daily, we will become planted like trees beside living waters and we will never run dry nor become unproductive, regardless of the change of seasons. How does this relate to our businesses? We want to be like that tree planted by the rivers of living water! We want to be EVERGREEN.

Businesses that lack concrete strategy are businesses that eventually cease to exist. We must be strategic in who we connect with, who we receive counsel from, and how we respond to success for our businesses to be successful in production. Take a moment to look around you. Who are you currently connected to?

Are these people bringing elevation or stagnation to your vision?

Who are you relying on to provide guidance and counsel concerning your next steps in business?

What results are you seeing as a result of receiving counsel from them?

If you find yourself very successful, what is your attitude towards those around you?

Have you become a know it all that takes all the credit and gives God none?

Strategy requires vision. Creating action steps will allow you to understand how to build capacity and sustainability in your business. It will allow you to create the culture that you desire in your workplace. Strategy will determine who becomes your advisors, who is hired as your assistant, and who you target as your consumer. We must commit to a vision that allows us to establish proper goals that allows us to focus on the success of our business while relying completely on God to direct our steps. Submit your vision and strategy to God and reap the harvest that you so rightfully deserve.

Prayer

Dear Heavenly Father,

I, (insert name) come to you first and foremost to say thank you. Thank you for leading and guiding me in all things. God, you have never left me nor forsaken me; for that, I say thank you. Thank you for trusting me with (insert business name). Without you, my business would not exist. God, I ask that you continue to provide me with rich vision concerning my life and business. Continue to connect me with godly, productive, and strategic people with willing hearts that are not only willing to connect with me but also collaborate and guide me in the strategies needed to continue to make business decisions that promote growth and sustainability. I come against every cultural barrier that would prevent me from penetrating the marketplace in an effective way. I call forth strong foundations and continued success. Help me to overcome weaknesses by building upon my strengths and finding hope in all opportunities. I will fear no threats or the thought of competition. Lord trust me to carry and bring forth witty ideas and profound inventions. Let me see pass that which only my physical eyes can see. Give me the sight needed to grasp the need of my clients and build accordingly. Don't let me become weary in my well doing; help me to continue to acknowledge you, Lord. I trust you to direct my path in all things—order my steps in you Lord. Let my feet be firmly planted and my hands diligent to perform in passion and purpose. May my heart find cheer in the creativity that you are bestowing upon me right now. I thank you God for innovative tools and resources—for placing my name and (insert business name) name in rooms I know not of. Thank you for orchestrating new resolutions and solutions in this season of my business. I bind myself to evergreen productivity. Lack of finances or consumer commitments will not come nigh my business. The economy will not influence my production nor limit my influence in the marketplace. God I am trusting you for overflow. Success is my portion. I thank you now, in Jesus' name. Amen.

The Source vs. The Resources

Elisha Lison

Peace I leave with you, my peace I give unto you: not as the world giveth, give
I unto you. Let not your heart be troubled, neither let it be afraid.
John 14:27 (KJV)

s a woman of faith and a woman in business, it's important to always stand on your faith and to remember who your source is in every situation and circumstance. I say this because as you go into business or if you are an entrepreneurial veteran, you will get familiar with the difficulties of entrepreneurship. As I fully stepped into allowing the Spirit to lead and guide my life and business, my mind would often flood with worry because of the uncertainty of finances. It was one thing to go from having what felt like security, when I knew the check was coming every other week, to stepping out on faith into the fear of the unknown. It took me months and a lot of going through cycles to receive one of the biggest revelations I have received to date. I realized that when I believe in my heart that God is my source for everything I need and want; I lack nothing, and I have full power over any situation or circumstance.

Jesus tells us in John 14:27 (KJV), "Peace I leave with you, my peace I give unto you: not as the world giveth, give I unto you. Let not your heart be troubled, neither let it be afraid." After allowing financial circumstances and situations to control my mood and emotions time after time, I asked God to reveal to me what was going on. He revealed to me that when my finances were good, I was good and, as my grandmother would say, when my money was funny, so was my mood. It would get me every single time and I couldn't shake it.

Now I knew I should turn to God when I encountered obstacles, but for some reason, when I encountered an obstacle, it felt like all my faith would leave and I did not even want to pray. The negative thoughts would roll in like a flood and it would get me so down that I wouldn't accomplish anything. I would constantly be on the verge of giving up. God made me aware of this cycle that was happening in my life. He revealed to me I was putting my power and joy in money and situations and not Him. So, when my finances were not adding up, my mood would reflect that. This was a poverty mindset and a generational hold that I decided must stop with me. When I realized that money should not be the deciding factor, whether I felt powerful or powerless, things really shifted.

When we walk around thinking money gives us our power and worth, we are releasing our power to it. It is imperative to know that God is our source of all our power, success. Joy and money is just the resource not the source. God created us with the ability to create wealth. He would not tell us to leave an inheritance for our children's children if He did not create us with the ability to do so.

This took a huge weight off my shoulders and allowed me to take my power back. I now know without a doubt that I can change any situation I am in; especially financially. He has given us everything we need, and then some, to live a more abundant life. We lack nothing in the Kingdom of Heaven. It is our inheritance to have everything we want and need and then some. I started seeking Him in the times where things were not adding up and asking Him to give me directions on how to change things around. He has blessed me with the blueprint that does not just benefit me, but generations after me.

Remember, you have access to all the answers by having access to God. You can overcome adversity with understanding and wisdom through our creator. Do not allow finances or situations to overcome you. You are a hyper conqueror in the mighty name of Jesus Christ!

Prayer

Father God in the name of Jesus, I ask that you open my eyes to the power that you have placed in me. The power to create wealth, the power to live life more abundantly and to shift my focus from lack and to the abundance that you have given me. Teach me how to live life more abundantly in every area of my life. Teach me how to walk in the power that you have placed within me and to never allow a situation or circumstance to steal my power again. You have already blessed me to have the answer to every adverse situation I am facing, and I trust you will lead and guide my footsteps to walk into the answer. I know that whatever I do shall prosper and I will not be afraid to step into the fullness of the potential that you have placed within me. Bring back to me the things that I have hidden and show me the things I have in my hands already to live this life in the fullness that you want me to. Bless my mind to be strategic and my hands to be fruitful and in Jesus' name, I pray. Amen.

Be Silent;
It's a Gift

Darlene Higgs Hollis

For thus says the Lord God, the Holy One of Israel: "In returning and rest you shall be saved; In quietness and confidence shall be your strength." But you would not..

Isaiah 30:15

How many of us are operating in chaos? Running around all day; constantly on the go. Burning the candle at both ends. Helping everyone that you can; even those not assigned to you. Busy, busy, busy. Not taking time to sit still. You feel stagnant in your life and business because there is so much clamor in your mind and spirit. When was the last time you really rested?

Years ago, while feeling so overwhelmed and living on fumes, I picked up my Bible one day, and it seemed to have just opened itself up to Isaiah 30:15. I sat there in shock! I knew God was using this scripture to speak straight to me! It was like, "Sit down and be quiet. Rest. And then you can hear me and get clarity." That day, I took time to sit in stillness and the next few weeks I pulled myself away from ministry and anything else I was doing so that I could just be STILL. This was a time of refreshing for me. I was able to make shifts in my life and gain clarity on the shift to make in my business. The gift of being quiet also gave me the confidence to create, build and wait for the opportune time to launch a business offer without telling anyone my vision in advance.

There is a gift in pausing. There is a gift for resting. You see clearly and can move forward with more confidence. You will not be easily moved. I can attest that when you rest, when you take time to be silent, you will feel stronger in your mind, body and your spirit. You will be ready to make decisions more confidently for your life and business. The icing on the cake when you step back is when you come back on the scene, you are ready to blaze your trail!

If you haven't yet, take time to rest and be still.

Prayer

Lord, you have been trying to speak to me, to give me instructions and insight, but I have been so busy I have not heard you. Today, I take this moment to retreat, be quiet and hear from you in the stillness. I take this time today to just rest. My mind needs this. My spirit needs this. My body needs this. Help me be okay with the quiet and the stillness. Help me be okay with spending time with myself. Be with me as I take time away to work in quiet. Help me set boundaries and only allow in my space what I need in this moment. I declare I will come out stronger because of this time I am taking to be quiet. I thank you in advance for all the gifts I will receive as a result of my obedience in making this space in my life. In Jesus' name I pray. Amen!

About the Co-Authors

Altovise Pelzer

Altovise Pelzer unmutes the voice of women who are ready to speak up about the things that have kept her silent for way too long. She is the founder of the *World Voice League, LLC*. Altovise also hosts *The #Speak-Easy Podcast*, allowing her to interview and collaborate with hundreds of CEOs, Speakers, and Creatives.

Altovise was honored as the *SpeakerCon 2021* Speaker on the Rise and holds the *Indie Author Legacy 2019 Award* for ebook of the year. Featured in magazines like *Courageous Woman Magazine*, *SwagHer Magazine*, and *UpWords Magazine*, she shares a story of inspiration and consistency. Hundreds of girls, women, and men have been unmuted in some way through the books, speeches, interviews, and coaching that Altovise has been committed to over the years.

Altovise is the Visionary Author for the #1 Best Selling books *"A Stage of Their Own: More Than a Movement"* and *"#Unmuted: Strategies to Move from Tragedy to Triumph"*. She is also a contributing author to the #1 Best Selling book *"Speak Up! The Ultimate Guide to Dominate in the Speaking Industry."* World-renowned speaking legends Dr. George Fraser and Les Brown wrote the Foreword and Afterword for the book.

Homelessness and molestation affected Altovise. She hit a turning point in her personal life after decades of being silent about her molestation story, even after finding out both her girls were molested. This was the catalyst for her decision to motivate women to "Leverage Their Life's Circumstances" by learning that their story was both valid and valuable.

Angela McGowan

Angela McGowan is a Professional Health Advocate who teaches and encourages each of her clients to stop being a doctor's patient who is not involved in their own patient care. Her real purpose and passion is to educate and enable patients to step into a new area and position of becoming a Powerful Patient!

A Powerful Patient is Positive, Passionate, Prepared, Persistent and on Purpose! When it comes to healthcare advocacy Angela is relentless in the pursuit of excellence for every patient, whether they are a client or not! She's very passionate about serving the healthcare needs of others! She prepares the patients and navigates them to a place that they can handle by asking the "RIGHT" questions of all medical providers!

As a Caregiving Strategy Consultant Angela's mission is to educate caregivers in 2 major ways:

1)   Instruct them on how to strategically implement techniques and tips, enabling them to give excellent care to those that they love. This instills calmness in the patient and confidence in the caregiver.

2)   Encouragement and the okay to not only think about but remember to love and care for themselves as well!

The "5" self-care areas the caregivers need to experience are physical, emotional, psychological, relational, and spiritual self-care!

Angela has over 25 years of experience in every facet of dealing with patients and their families within healthcare administration, insurance claims as well as authorizations. She is very active in healthcare advocacy and is the founder of Angie's P.A.C.E. [Patient Advocates Committed to Excellence}; the facilitator of the Powerful Patient Movement Facebook group; the Host of the weekly FB show "Say-It" Sunday" and the author and publisher of all her books the latest is the creation of The Patient Blueprint Planner!

Angela McGowan is a Christian Entrepreneur, Encourager, Intercessor, Success Mentor and Visionary! She has 2 adult daughters, Andrea and Adrianne. She also has 2 grandchildren, Anthony-Ray and Aniya Monae, who are the Joy of her life! She enjoys traveling between three states for business and to see family and friends.

When you connect with Angela as a Professional Healthcare Advocate, she'll help you achieve excellent medical care and become a powerful patient on your health care journey!

Additionally, you can also connect with her as a Caregiver Strategy Consultant! Creating strategies that will allow the caregiver to ease into the process, which will help them to prepare to go into the role either full or part time.

Angela has created several products that work in partnership with her books: *How to Get Out of the Hospital ALIVE; 911 Caregiver Down*; and the *Patient Blueprint Planner*, along with her video workshop, "How to Prepare to Medically Raise Your Parents"!
This fall she will release her *Men's Health Book*!

Anitra Truelove

Anitra Truelove lives her life in pursuit of one overall calling. That calling being to demonstrate the prophetic mandate of turning the hearts of fathers back to the children and the children's hearts back to their fathers [so our land will be healed and not cursed (Malachi 4:6)]. In 2008, she was ordained as a prophet and in the same year became the founder of Healing Waters Ministry Inc. Anitra applied her expertise gained in music entertainment, multimedia, and non-profit organizational industries to offer a gathering in her hometown to create a safe prophetic atmosphere for young people to be healed, delivered, and trained in Kingdom movement and to be activated in their purpose and identity. This year Anitra was joined in holy matrimony to Chitonio. Together they have five wonderful children. The Trueloves are Life and Business Coaches specializing in relationships and youth. They are also called to reform nations.

Blessing Shuman

Blessing is a native of Savannah, GA, currently living in the Dallas/Ft. Worth area. She is married to her best friend, Frederick Shuman, Jr and is most importantly a friend of Jesus Christ. In 2004, she began her college career at Georgia Southern University but returned home to graduate from Armstrong Atlantic State University, where she earned a Bachelor of Liberal Arts, minoring in Psychology. She also completed several courses towards her Masters in Christian Counseling from Liberty University.

In pursuit of finances during and after college, she worked in retail for almost 10 years. This afforded her the opportunity not only to dress women of different sizes and shapes, but to learn different patterns and techniques to help them look their best aesthetically. She believes fashion is more than just putting on nice clothes but encouraging women to believe that they are absolutely beautiful just as they are, embracing their current while they are on the way to their personal goals.

After working 5 years at a Fortune 500 Logistics company, she decided to launch her dream, Embrace.

Career Highlights Include: Featured by Ashley Stewart, Gabrielle Union, and NY&Co for outfits styled; Hosted in-store events for Ashley Stewart, Lane Bryant, and LOFT; WSAV News Appearance airing Embrace Beauty Blessing Initiative; Fashion Conversationalist at Boost Brunch 2019; Business Networking Brunch Panelist for Fashion;

Master Stylist and curation assistant for the WTAL Virtual Experience Boutique and ILS Apparel Collection.

She currently serves as a Mentor Navigator with New Day Services, empowering mothers with tools to encourage their self-worth. Blessing is also a Certified Life Coach specializing in Confidence Coaching.

Brandi Rojas

Pastor Brandi L. Rojas is a native of Greensboro, N.C. She serves with her Husband, Pastor Omar Rojas at Maximizing Life Family Worship Center in Greensboro, N.C., a vision God birthed through them in 2015. Rojas has been in Dance Ministry for over 20 years and is a 2009 graduate of the School of Disciples taught under the late Bishop Otis Lockett, Sr.; in 2013, she was named Sweetheart of the Triad, an award given based on community involvement. Pastor Rojas was licensed to preach the Gospel on February 27, 2011, and as a result DYmondFYre Global Ministries was born. Rojas was ordained as an Elder June 22, 2012 and was installed as Pastor with her Husband on January 27, 2013.

Since that time, she and her Husband, also known as #TeamRojas, by God's mandate, have birthed several evangelistic causes. In January 2014, Rojas opened FYreDance Studios and Liturgical Arts Consulting which provides on-site instruction, virtual teaching, consultation services, choreography services and dance encounters. The following year, a prayer walk initiative was created to bring the local churches and community together to collaborate and help lead the lost to Jesus Christ and empower the world through a vehicle called The Gatekeeper's Legacy. Since that time, she has also served as part of the planning and leadership committee for the National Day of Prayer in the City of Greensboro and currently serves as the youngest committee member, only African-American and only female on the core team.

In February 2016, Rojas launched out again to begin IgniteHerSoul International Women's Fellowship (formerly The Legacy Ladies Fellowship), an organization created to help women of God pray, push and live the reality of what God has called them to. The CrossOver Resource Center was later birthed out of the mandate of Maximizing Life FWC, which works to provide solutions for life's transitions to the community. Rojas released her first book in June 2016, entitled *In the Face of Expected Failure* and her sophomore project, *Humpty Dumpty in Stilettos: The Great Exchange*, in November 2016. It was with the second book releasee that Fiery Beacon Publishing House, LLC was launched, serving current and upcoming authors, playwrights and poets. Since that time, she along with her FBPH Team have been able to help over 115 authors launch and pursue their literary dreams, along with owning the first Author Incubator Hub, "The Ink Lab," giving literary creatives a safe place to think and CREATE. *Humpty Dumpty in Stilettos* was nominated for the National Literary Trailblazer of the Year Award in 2017 by the Indie Author Legacy Award in Baltimore, Maryland, and in July 2017, she was noted as an International Best-Selling Author for her part in a collaborative effort called *Stories from the Pink Pulpit: Women in Ministry Speak*.

Chanel Blackmore

Chanel Blackmore has dedicated her years to bringing out the best in a people, especially women, purposefully. A former corporate trainer, published author, minister, and a remarkable certified Life coach, Chanel draws upon her 15 years' experience from the field of education to a career path where she can drive and empower women to pursue their true identities. With firsthand knowledge of what self-authenticity entails, Chanel inspired JustBMore Coaching, an organization whose mission is to sharpen, encourage, and motivate women in every area of life.

In her community, she is widely recognized as the "purpose pusher" for her uncanny ability to spot areas which steal their uniqueness and support them with a great passion for maximizing their newly found unique self. Chanel is the author of two motivational books, *What's In Your Box* and *Watch me Werk*. She was a co-host of an online talk show, *BYOB Morning Show* and you can find some of her ministerial videos on YouTube. Also, Chanel has mounted the podium at several events to shed more light on the topic of women putting themselves first.

As a coach, she designs her workshops, events, and courses to precisely guide these women through self-discovery and reflection. Chanel is one coach who drives you to discover what you are most passionate about, and in turn live successfully and soulfully.

Learn more about Chanel:
www.chanelblackmore.com
https://www.facebook.com/justbmore/
https://www.facebook.com/ChanelBlackmore
https://www.linkedin.com/in/chanel-blackmore/

Speaking Moments:
https://coachingcouses.s3.us-east-2.amazonaws.com/Chanel+Blackmore+Social+01.mp4
https://coachingcouses.s3.us-east-2.amazonaws.com/Chanel+Blackmore+-+All+In+-+2019-07-15_1.mp4

Coleen Ifill Nipper

Coleen Nipper, a native of New York, serves as the Senior Pastor of Total Praise Worship Center Inc. in Atlanta GA.

As the Director of Early Learning, she provides support to four Head Start programs in several states. She has many years of experience conducting professional development training, teacher onboarding, working with various school districts, and collaborating with mental health and disability coordinators.

Being raised in a Christian home, Coleen was always involved in ministry. She knew at an early age that she was called to teach. Coleen's passion for teaching grew enormously, which led her to become a Sunday school teacher. Coleen also served as a youth Pastor, praise and worship leader, and Ordained Evangelist.

Coleen's obedience and reverence to the Lord is one thing that have sustained her and allowed her to continue to humble herself in her ministry walk. She thanks God for her two children Chelsea and Zhalil. Her favorite passage in the Bible would be Psalm 27:4 "One thing have I desired of the LORD, that will I seek after; that I may dwell in the house of the LORD all the days of my life, to behold the beauty of the LORD, and to enquire in his temple. She knows without a doubt that all the days of her life have been worth every battle and test and can't wait to see what the Lord has in store for her next dimension.

Dorothea 'Thea' Robinson

"If I had a gun, I would kill you!"

Those cutting words became motivation for a strategic plan of escape. After her silent exodus, Amazon Best Selling author, international speaker, Domestic Violence Advocate, Advocate Trainer and Life Coach, Dorothea Thea Robinson (X-It Strategist) began a global effort immersed in strategically planning safe passage for women fleeing intimate partner abusive relationships. She is founder of the Butterfly Experience: one more butterfly freed and LADV (Life After Domestic Violence), where she coaches victims, survivors and advocates on discovering who they truly are, and moving them to their life's call. Whether in the development of escape planning, Life Coaching or creating business models, individuals will recognize their self-worth.

Dorothea hosts the LADV Podcast, is author of "Ah Ha", co-author of *The Butterfly Experience: one more butterfly freed*, and co- author of Amazon Best Seller, "A Stage of Their Own". This Philadelphian is also a mother of six while developing programs to assist advocates to reach their fullest potential in business. Dorothea's free time consists of cooking, reading, and enjoying family time.

Dorothea T Robinson's goal is to ensure that "One more butterfly is freed".

Learn more about Dorothea:

bit.ly/talkwiththea

Elisha Lison

"When I lost everything, I knew I had to make some changes, so I became. Now, I am on a life mission to help others do the same thing." Elisha is a proud mother of two children and the Founder of Laced & Layered Hair Company. She is obtaining her Bachelor of Divinity degree and a certification as a Life & Business Coach. Elisha says, "Now, I am currently writing my best piece of work, my life."

Learn more about Elisha:

https://lacedandlayeredhairco.com
https://www.facebook.com/LLHairCo/

Dr. Janine Graham-Howard

An anointed preacher, teacher, motivator, encourager, investor, leader, prophet, transformational specialist, and an accomplished author. Executive Pastor at Abundant Mercy Christian Church International McDonough, GA with her husband, Apostle Robert Howard Jr., Senior Servant Pastor. Dr. Janine is also Dean and Adjunct Professor at Abundant Mercy Bible Institute. Dr. Janine is the CEO and visionary of Living for His Purpose National Women's Ministry. Coaching women to Live, Laugh, Love and Dream on Purpose. Encouraging God's people to STOP Existing and START Living. Business owner of *Confidence Academy* and *I AM… Life Coach Academy.*

Dr. Janine has been an RN for the last 32 years, specializing mostly in critical care. Caring is part of her genuine nature. She has a Master's in Divinity and PhD. Dr. Janine is a Certified Life Coach and counselor. A healthy mind, body and soul is important to her ministry. Live your best life now.

Learn more about Dr. Janine:
> drjaninemin@gmail.com
> drjanineministris.org
> FB @DrJanine Graham Howard
> IG @drjaninemidwife

Keisa Campbell

Keisa epitomizes femininity, resilience, women's empowerment, and beautiful living. Crowned Ms. Georgia 2019 in the Mr. & Mrs. Black America Pageant, Keisa is the founder and CEO of Beautiful Living, a holistic wellness brand created to impact, inspire and help women of faith live more fulfilling lives.

Keisa is a life strategist, speaker, image consultant, and author with over 20 years of experience transforming women's lives. She is a certified professional life and beauty coach with a Bachelor's in Business Administration. Featured in *Voyage Atl* and *Shoutout Atlanta*, Keisa is committed to helping women identify purpose, and obtain healthy relationships and mindsets.

Learn more about Keisa:

www.keisacampbell.com

Kelina Morgan

Kelina is a life coach, business coach, and minister. She is a graduate of the University of Minnesota with a degree in Social Work, Sociology, and Youth Studies. She also attended Life Christian University in Charlotte, NC with studies in Christian Counseling. Kelina has an over 20-year career in mental health where she has focused on ending homelessness for those who experience mental illness. Kelina is a minister at Fellowship Church in Woodbury, MN where Pastor Timothy Brewington II presides.

At age 3, her family moved from the impoverished East St. Louis for a better life and opportunity. Family was often the only support system, so she grew up very close to her extended family as they sometimes had to live together and eat together to get by. Her grandmother turned no one away, no matter how full the house or how many needed to be fed. This humility and love for others is a trait that she has also received.

Kelina, an overcomer, and chain-breaker has survived sexual violence as a child and adult, domestic abuse, low self-esteem, depression, PTSD, betrayal, manipulation by leadership, poverty, divorce, and single motherhood. Kelina is a fighter and resilient, with the tenacity to overcome life's obstacles and come out better. Kelina's purpose is to support women who have experienced discouragement, disappointment, and low self-esteem with moving forward into life and purpose. In her own words, "I see those who often go unseen. I see the hurt, the shame, the disappointment, the low self-esteem, and the self-doubt that so many walk around with and I am called to support those who desire to be whole in Christ.

Find out more about Kelina at www.kmchain-breaker.org

Kenria Kelly

As a Life and Business Coach, Kenria was an entrepreneur in the beauty and fashion industry long before God called her to frontline ministry; she ministered to and counselled women and men from all walks of life with their personal and family challenges. After suffering four miscarriages and navigating through a painful divorce the Lord led her into a life of deep devotion in prayer, consecration and service that birthed a Prophetic, Deliverance and Healing Mantle. She has been called a Revivalist and Prayer Strategist with a breaker anointing. to birth both personal revival and restoration to those who have been rejected, broken and outcast.

The Lord has called her to the nations ministering throughout the length and breadth of the Bahama Islands the Caribbean, the United States and indeed the world. Kenria believes it is of utmost importance to know how you have been called and to whom you have called to be effective in your assignment.

Her life and ministry have been birthed and evolved through the power of prayer!

Learn more about Kenria: https://prophetesskenriakelly.com

Laquanda Whitehead-Grady

Minister Laquanda Whitehead-Grady accepted Christ as her Lord and Savior at 13. She received her Bachelor of Science in Agriculture from The Fort Valley State (College) University, Fort Valley, Georgia in 1996. In December 2000, she acknowledged her call to the ministry. In December 2003, she was consecrated as a licensed minister. In 2005, she was asked to serve as an instructor to assist in the training and preparation of ministers for ordination. Feeling the unction of the Lord to learn more about God's Word, she attended Liberty University, Lynchburg, Virginia, where she earned her Master of Arts in Religion in Evangelism and Church Planting in 2008. In 2016, she was asked to become the female instructor in the newly established Church of God by Faith Theological Seminary (CTI). Later, she was promoted to Director of Christian Teaching Certification Program for the Seminary. She became an ordained minister in 2019.

By profession, she is an entrepreneur and the owner of *LQ's Desktop Publishing, LLC*. She is happily married to Pastor Stacey D. Grady Sr. besides ministerial duties and tasks, she also serves alongside her husband as co-Pastor. And together they have two beautiful girls, Stacey Devon II and Kendrick Kevon, ages 8 and 6, respectively.

Latesha Higgs

Latesha Higgs, a Baltimore native and member of Delta Sigma Theta Sorority, Inc., is a podcaster who has been seen and heard on multiple platforms speaking and advocating for those living with a mental health condition and suicide prevention. As a speaker and advocate, she shares her lived experiences of surviving her brother's death by suicide as well as personally managing Bipolar 2 disorder. By employing scripture, therapy, and medication to live a life of recovery, she inspires others to do the same through teaching, mentoring, and coaching. Latesha currently teaches and lives in the Atlanta Metro area of Georgia and serves as the President/Executive Director of the *DIVA Effect, Inc.*—a nonprofit she found in 2016. In May 2019, the *DIVA Effect, Inc.* became one of several Community Champions for Maryland's *2019 Children's Mental Health Matters Campaign* and hosted several free activities and events during *Children's Mental Health Awareness Week.* In 2019, under the leadership of psychiatrist Dr. Daniel Hale, the Special Advisor to the Office of the President at Johns Hopkins Bayview Medical Center, Latesha was one of the founding members of the *Congregational Depression Awareness Program* in Baltimore, Maryland. For her service to the community, Latesha has won multiple awards from various organizations, including from the Gamma Omicron Omega Chapter of Iota Phi Theta Fraternity, Inc. More of Latesha's story can be found in *Voyage Atl* online magazine.

M'rcedes Jones

M'rcedes Dioné, is a mother of two boys and one angel baby! She's a makeup artist, a holistic esthetician and business owner. She is launching her own cosmetics line.

She is also an intercessor and deliverance minister that operates in the prophetic heavily. She has a heart to see everyone from all walks of life healed and full of peace.

She feels her purpose in life is to ensure women walk in the confidence God has given them. Beauty is more than makeup and it stems from the love we feel within ourselves. She calls herself the Confidence BuildHER!

Learn more about M'rcedes: https://mrcedesdione.square.site/

Monique Caradine-Kitchens

Monique Caradine-Kitchens has a very clear mission: to help as many women as possible create generational wealth.

In 2018, Monique launched a company that is now known as *Over-Flow Enterprises LLC*. Under this entity she is expanding her brand as an author, podcaster, trainer and Certified Money Breakthrough Coach for women leaders and entrepreneurs.

She is the host of the *Sisternomics Podcast*, and her book is entitled *How to Embrace Your Inner Millionaire*.

She uses her nearly two decades as an on-air personality and entrepreneur, to help women heal their relationship with money, monetize their expertise, get visibility and create generational wealth.

From 1997 until 2012, Monique held on-air positions at both WVON Radio in Chicago and My50 Chicago (a FOX affiliate). She hosted and produced community-focused programs and became known as one of the top talk show hosts in the nation.

Monique has been featured on dozens of podcasts and the top national media outlets including CNN, National Public Radio, FOX News, ESSENCE Magazine, SIRIUS XM Satellite Radio, the Chicago Tribune, Black Enterprise.com and many more. Her *Sisternomics* podcast is listened to in over 50 countries worldwide and ranked in the top 3% of podcasts globally.

Learn more about Monique: www.OverflowNow.com

Pretina Lowery

Pretina originally from Brooklyn, New York, at the tender age of twenty, she traveled cross-country to take up residency in San Diego, California.

Pretina lived there until 2011 and moved to Las Vegas, Nevada. She currently lives in the state of Georgia.

She is the mother of three daughters and is blessed to be called Gigi by her five grandchildren.

Pretina is a poet, songwriter, standup comedian, facilitator, transformation strategy consultant and published author.

Pretina recently released her seventh book entitled *Knee Mail 40 Days of Purposeful Prayer* and is currently working on her eighth book.

Pretina is a social butterfly, enjoys gathering with others and views no one as a stranger, only someone to be loved and celebrated.

Pretina has spoken at Women's Conferences, Youth retreats, birthday and homegoing celebrations. She realized at a very young age she loved teaching. This passion has allowed her to mentor middle school, high school and young adults at the various stages of their lives.

Pretina founded the *Source Center* to assist women and children as they transition through difficult seasons and situations in life.

Pretina fully understands that prayer is a privilege and prides herself in the perpetual act of making her petitions and requests known to the God who is well able to answer.

Ronisa Glass

Ronisa S. Glass is a native Atlantan, educated in APS and a graduate of Bryman Institute-National Education Center, where she earned her Medical Assistant Certification and has worked in the medical field for more than 28 years.

Ronisa was first licensed as a minister in 2009. Even furthering the call of ministry upon her life, she was chosen to begin an extensive training program for the Apostolic Team, of Passion for Worship Ministries International. In February of 2017, she was ordained into the Five-Fold Office of Teacher. Ronisa was also ordained as an Elder at Embassy International Worship Center in Jan of 2019. She has faithfully served in ministry in many areas.

In 2014, she launched Fireproof Ministries, which is a ministry geared towards helping women who've gone through any form of brokenness, to know that they don't have to carry the residue of what they've gone through. Her passion for helping women is the driving force behind her 4E System, which is to Encourage, Edify, Educate & Empower women to come up and come out of any form of brokenness. No matter how difficult the circumstances that came her way, she was able to stand and make it through.

Learn more about Ronisa: www.iamronisaglass.com

Dr. Roz Knighten-Warfield

Dr. Roz Knighten-Warfield is the CSO (Chief Smile Officer) for *Stop It & Smile, Roz Knighten-Warfield LLC.*, and publishing company *Scribe & Write*. Roz is an amazon best-selling author of multiple books, international speaker, relational currency strategist, coach/mentor, wordsmith creator, and prayer warrior. She is the visionary of clubhouse club *Trucking God's Way*. She is certified by Coach Academy International. She passionately enjoys collaborative measures and effective partnerships amongst men & women who desire to lead lives full of zeal, clarity and courage. Roz believes in Living Your Best Life and S.O.A.R (Surrendered, Obedient, Abiding, Radically). Roz has been a part of the corporate and plus years. She is equipped with consulting, project management, and customer service engagement to empower, encourage, elevate, enlighten, and educate thoughts of imagination to fulfill dreams, vision, and goals. Roz is your #1 campaigner. She seeks out the good in others. Dr. Roz is married to the love of her life Vincent Warfield and resides in Dallas, Tx

Contact Dr. Roz Knighten- Warfield: easyroz60@gmail.com
Website: https://rozknightenwarfield.com

Shaundra Straughter

A Georgia native, Shaundra Straughter is a devoted educator, minister, certified life and business coach, blogger, wife and mom. A dynamic servant-leader and Christian; she possesses a host of talents but finds fulfillment in carrying out her purpose as God's servant. In the summer of 2020, she became the founder of The Faith Stir, LLC. Being a firm believer that all things should be done in a spirit of excellence, she began perfecting her craft and curating her content for her next level of service, life and business coaching. She hosted her first successful virtual women's coaching retreat Mirror Me Success in 2021. She enjoys hosting podcast sessions via her business page on Facebook. There her audience can find laughter, practical keys to success, and transparency in her struggles and victories.

Learn more about Shaundra: https://www.thefaithstir.com.

Tenishia B. Lester

Tenishia B. Lester is a Certified International Master Life/Business Coach, Certified International Christian Coach, Certified Pastoral Counselor, Author, and Speaker.

Tenishia B. Lester Enterprises, LLC enables Tenishia to coach entrepreneurial minded women who are ready to overcome self-defeating mindsets and behaviors to become more self-aware to live tenacious bold lives.

Raised in New Jersey, Tenishia currently resides in Georgia. She is the proud mother of one son (another preceded her in death) and a grandson. As a result of experiencing years of childhood sexual abuse, not being secure in her identity or knowing her life's purpose, imposter syndrome, low-self-esteem and other issues. Tenishia made up her mind to change the trajectory of her life. Tenishia is an advocate for counseling and healing ministries as it has helped her during the lowest moments of her life. In addition, to counseling and healing ministries, Tenishia had the assistance of a Life Coach to help her navigate life circumstances. Therefore, she knows the value of life coaching firsthand.

Her book *Arrested Development: A Journey to Discovering Identity and Purpose* was penned and birthed during her healing process. Tenishia's heart behind her book is to provide a resource that gives insight and hope to those who are or have experienced childhood trauma, life challenges and/or lack of identity and purpose.

Tenishia realized that her struggles were not for her during her healing process, but for the uplifting of others. With a heart to lead and serve, Tenishia finds joy in enlightening, empowering, encouraging, and teaching others how to change their story. Tenishia is passionate and committed to seeing others win. Her compassionate caring ways and her listening ear positions Tenishia as one who is sought out by many to assist them by providing wisdom and guidance in life. Her creativity has afforded women with businesses to create products and services, to enhance revenue.

Tenishia is proof of what freedom looks like and that you too can overcome adversity. Her Motto is "Healing....it's a whole journey, not a destination;" one that she is committed to going on with others.

Learn more about Tenishia: www.tenishiablester.com
Social Media: @tenishiablester1

TuRhonda Freeman

TuRhonda Freeman is Founder + Chief Encouragement Officer at Sanctum + Seed. She's a dream-chasing, faith-pushing, ministry leader and entrepreneur who wants to see believers thrive in every season of life. Whether she's hosting a podcast, teaching a bible study, writing, or even coaching leaders, TuRhonda shares a dual passion for both ministry and business. Having spent the last decade in the franchise industry, she retired from the business in order to focus primarily on vision projects, legacy building and purposeful living with her husband Jerry. Together, they operate a real estate investing business and make their home in Lawrenceville, GA with their daughter Jade Ivy.

As a visionary, TuRhonda creates purposeful products for her brand Sanctum + Seed, such as the Write the Vision! Board, affirmation cards and journals. As a writer and Bible teacher, TuRhonda's personal mission is to see the Word of God take root in ordinary people like herself. She is the author of the Sanctum + Seed bible study journal, "Deborah, Arise!" and a new book entitled "Anchored", set to release in Fall 2022.

Learn more about TuRhonda: www.sanctumandseed.com

ABOUT THE VISIONARY AUTHOR

Darlene Higgs Hollis, a Certified Master Life & Business Coach, the founder of the *Rebranding My Life* movement for women, and an ordained minister and founder of *Broken Silence Ministries*. She is passionate about being a midwife for women birthing their dreams. She holds Bachelor's degrees in Biology and Chemistry and a Master of Public Health.

She is an Amazon Best-Selling Author of six books: *Divorced 'Suddenly Single' Mom's Devotional, Divorced "Suddenly Single" Mom's Devotional 2, Rebranding 'Notes to Self' Journal, Rebranding My Life Anthology, Crisis in Paradise: 9 Women's Experience During Hurricane Dorian Anthology* and *#Unmuted: Strategies to Move From Tragedy to Triumph Anthology* (co-author).

As the CEO of DH Book Consulting & Publishing, a publisher for women, most of her clients call her their "Book Midwife." She uses all of her professional qualifications and experiences, as well as her personal experience of overcoming various traumatic life experiences, to successfully help them give birth to their book baby.

Darlene is especially passionate about women breaking their silence and putting it in print to leave their stamp on this earth. She strives to ensure that every author preserves her voice as she writes and publishes her book.

A Certified Master Life & Business Coach Trainer, she is also the Founder and lead instructor of *Rebranding My Life International Coaching*

Academy, where she trains women how to follow their passion by becoming Life & Business Coaches.

In 2020, during the pandemic, Darlene gave birth to *MariBelle Vané Beauty*, a skincare line named to honor the memory of her three sisters, Marion, Isabelle and Vanessa.

She has been featured in several media outlets, including *Courageous Women Magazine, BahamasLocal.com, Native Stew,* and *The Bahamas Weekly.*

Learn more about Darlene:

www.dhbooksandpublishing.com
www.thecprlifecoach.com
www.rmlicoachingacademy.com

Facebook: Darlene Hollis -The CPR Life Coach
Instagram: @darlenehiggshollis

Made in the USA
Middletown, DE
08 February 2023

24307139R00109